HIGH-PERFORMANCE EXECUTIVE LEADERSHIP

For Senior Executives Responsible
For Delivering World-Class
Organisational Performance

High-Performance Executive Leadership

❖

10 Surprising Myths That
Senior Executive Must Break
To Avoid Irrelevance

EMMA SHARROCK

**The Trusted Authority To Senior Executives
On Creating High-Performance Cultures**

Published By Agile Enterprises / High Performance Culture Partners

Address: Level 9, 440 Collins Street Melbourne VIC 3000
Website: www.HighPerformanceCulturePartners.com.au

PRAISE FOR THE AUTHOR

"Emma thrives in the fast-paced world in which we live, brimming with energy, enthusiasm and a natural talent for spotting better ways of doing things.

She is gifted in her ability to read the situation in which we are operating and to lead people to understand how best to turn those circumstances to their advantage both through individual endeavours and through the strong leadership of others. Emma inspires with her passion and her ability to help others seek to improve on the status quo."

Dr Erin Lalor, AM, Not-For-Profit CEO

"As a leader, I have seen firsthand Emma's incredible presence and contribution to supporting me build a higher-performing team.

I am acutely aware of the vulnerability that exists when bringing in an external party into sensitive team and stakeholder dynamics. Emma is able to navigate this complexity with aplomb, pragmatism and empathy, which enables diverse stakeholders to feel an instant connection and interest to actually engage with the process.

I appreciate Emma's no-nonsense approach to empower others to work together to find the solutions that will endure in their unique circumstances. It speaks to her genuine desire to bring people together to achieve remarkable outcomes when the odds are against them."

**Madeline Oldfield, Former Director
Resolving Disputes Digitally,
VCAT Melbourne**

"I've known Emma for 10 years, having first met her when we were studying together at the Australian Graduate School of Management. Emma has an inquiring mind—a razor-sharp intellect—and she gets business strategy as well as anyone I've worked with during my 18-year career at management level in financial services.

I've regularly sought Emma's advice and guidance on the full range of management and leadership challenges. More recently, I was thrilled to be able to secure her services to facilitate a critical design conversation capturing perspectives from five different organisations.

Emma's latest book promises to be an insightful guide for anyone looking to make a positive impact for their organisation."

Mark Morand, Head of Microenterprise and Insurance Good Shepherd Microfinance Melbourne

"Emma's magic is the ability to enter a room of people with differing agendas and engagement levels and to leave with that same group of people united around a common outcome and how it will be achieved. And once the 'how' is agreed, Emma changes gears to work with teams to ensure continued alignment on the delivery front. She is a true expert in Agile and is pragmatic in how she applies it.

With a facilitation toolkit that is deep and varied, I've observed Emma change her approach during workshops in response to the feeling in the room.

This cradle-to-grave approach to facilitation and coaching means Emma truly is one of a kind and is an incredibly valuable asset for any company."

Ellen Cresswell, Digital Technology Executive Melbourne

"One of the many privileges of leadership in the Australian Navy is the unique opportunity to meet and work with and alongside a number of extraordinary, extremely talented and enthusiastic young Australians willing to contribute to their country in the Australian Defence Force. I've found over the years, as time tends to blunt the memory that you tend to remember only those young Australians who are exceptionally talented or conversely those who have spectacularly ended their careers in a shower of sparks.

Emma is one of those exceptionally talented young leaders that I very clearly recall first meeting when she was a midshipman seeking guidance about a topic for her honours thesis at the Australian Defence Force Academy. She was confident and intensely focussed with an open, enquiring mind.

Her excellent sense of humour and well-developed interpersonal skills were enhanced by her impressive communication ability, all of which underpinned a quietly confident, effective leadership style. It was clear at the outset that this young officer possessed the personal qualities that would harbour success in any chosen career.

Some years later, Emma and I would serve briefly together in a Guided Missile Destroyer, where I was able to observe closely how the significant leadership challenges and experiences at sea had successfully developed her confidence and reinforced those positive personal qualities that were quite evident some years earlier. The sea-going environment had developed and shaped her talents and admirable qualities into that of a confident, extremely successful, competent and innovative leader.

Having made her contribution to the Australian Defence Force, Emma sought challenges outside the Defence Force, and some years later our paths crossed again on our respective private pilgrimages over the Owen Stanley Ranges, Papua New Guinea to the battlefields of Kokoda in 2008. It was at this stage that I discovered that Emma was confidently, successfully and cheerfully weaving her personal qualities and immense skill set into the discipline of project management in Melbourne.

Not long afterwards, Emma had (not surprisingly) launched her own company and successfully written her first book, The Agile Project Manager. She continues to excel in not only motivating teams but also in teaching others the skills and awareness of the art of motivation and successful leadership.

Emma's journey continues today as she effectively applies her impressive talents and outstanding personal qualities in the corporate world honed by experiences in some tough environments. This next book is yet another exclamation mark on another fabulous milestone of her extraordinarily successful career."

**Commodore Simon J. Hart,
CSC RAN (Retired)**

CONTENTS

INTRODUCTION

Y ou have picked up this book because you are a senior leader who is responsible for delivering strategic results that drive change, sustain growth and have a positive impact on your organisation's ability to perform in a rapidly changing economy. In addition, you seek to continually shape a high-performance culture that sustains this performance well into the future.

Without a doubt, you've worked hard to reach the position you're now at in your career. You've navigated these seas for many years. You're well-known and respected, so you feel ready to make a significant contribution to where your organisation lands on the economic coastline.

Turbulent Seas & Challenging Navigation

While your standards are high and you seek to reach levels that are beyond those expected of you, you've also noticed that the economic waters are filling up rapidly with competitors and that the wind patterns and currents are faster and less predictable. Your approach, your guidance system, which once worked well in the past, doesn't seem to be as effective at achieving your goals when navigating these uncharted waters.

Sure, you're following a proven strategic line of attack, but manoeuvres that worked in the past are just not effective anymore. Your ship seems like it is going in circles and you're struggling to find a way to set you and your team back on course. Smaller ships are passing you; they are faster and nimbler, with the ability to negotiate their way around obstacles with greater speed and dexterity, and they are reaching the economic coastline faster—capturing an increasing market share.

To perform at your best and keep up with changes as they emerge in this continually shifting environment, you feel that you need something more. A compass of sorts, that helps you and your team navigate your way through rougher seas and around economic obstacles so that you remain buoyant and moving forward at pace.

Steering Your Leader 'Ship' To Success

As a senior leader, you must perform at a high level, as must your team and those throughout your organisation. You're the captain of the ship, and your team are your crew. You need to work strategically in times of calm, and rally together when the waters become rough.

By bringing out the best in yourself and your team, you align their capabilities with your performance expectations, as well as those of your organisation, to promote smooth sailing in both calm and rough seas.

But how do you manage and improve the performance of your people, and instil a world-class achievement culture, all while keeping pace with the speed of change happening around you?

Getting clear answers to that question is the definitive 'compass' to your success. What has worked for you in the past is not going to work in the future. The future requires different thinking, an altered leader 'ship,' and a fundamental shift in what you know to be true right now. Those truths have rapidly become myths, surrounded by murky waters, and they need to be busted and unlearned to make way for new thinking, clearer water, and world-class performance.

How do I know this?

I have worked in the business of change and transformation for over 20 years. So, I've seen my share of adaptation and transition.

See, I started a career in the Royal Australian Navy as an Officer of the Watch where I governed the bridge, manoeuvred the ship in strategic and simulated warfare, and protected the crew. During this time, my leadership skills were continually tested.

One minute we'd be cruising through calm and friendly waters, and the next we'd be in amongst the enemy in simulated warfare, firing and avoiding torpedoes. Or I would be facing unexpected problems such as the ship's steering gear failing, a fire, or manoeuvring to recover a man overboard.

These opportunities allowed me to learn how to adapt my leadership in a fast-paced, ever-changing environment that ensured everyone on-board the ship was not only safe but performing to a high standard. So, collectively we created a world-class culture, one driven by a need to survive and succeed.

Every watch was a balance between the day-to-day management of a team and resolving urgent issues as they arose—all while being expected to continuously improve my leadership skills, progress in my career, and mentor my team members.

From The Bridge To The Boardroom

Since my time at sea, the pace of change for me as a leader has increased.

I may have moved from the bridge to the boardroom, but I still take on many challenges that are not unlike those I experienced as a military leader, except now I balance day to day delivery of complex change with urgent issues that need immediate resolution.

High performance was, and still is, a must, as is the ability to take others on a journey toward greater achievement. Yet, it's the rewards, both personal and professional, for succeeding during times of often turbulent change that make all the hard work worthwhile.

After delivering projects in my capacity as a project and program manager for many years, an opportunity surfaced that allowed me to transition both my skills and experience into a coaching role. Working under a mentor whom I admired gave me the opportunity to add greater magnitude to my knowledge and experience and also positioned me to help more people, across multiple projects and organisations, rather than focusing my energy on a single program of work.

This shift from one to many helped me develop an even greater appreciation of the pressures and challenges found in modern corporate life. Coaching many teams to perform at their best by unlearning their old thinking, and then applying a new, adaptive approach to work practices meant profound results on a larger scale.

But I soon discovered that it wasn't just the teams that needed to unlearn old thinking; it was also their leaders.

The change journey for an organisation without their leader on-board is like a ship sailing without its captain—the lack of a role model erodes the crew's ability, or, in this case, the team's ability, to visualise what high performance really is, and to ultimately perform at their best. With the leader fully on-board, buying-in and applying new thinking to how they lead their organisation, inspires everyone else to follow.

Over the years, I've naturally evolved from delivering programs of work for organisations to helping leaders and teams improve and refine how they lead change and produce powerful and ongoing results that see these organisations leave their mark economically.

Having now coached hundreds of people—teams, leaders, and organisations from transport to telecommunications to media and finance—in the art of delivering world-class results and improving performance by applying simple yet effective strategies, it's now time for me to turn my attention towards you.

From Truth To Myths

Strategies begin by understanding the underlying beliefs that are the foundations of your life. These beliefs become truths that have undoubtedly got you to where you are now, but, unfortunately, will get you no further.

Why?

Well, these truths are no longer true. They have become myths—and, just like the stuff of legends, they make for an interesting story but will not lead to high performance in a world that is fast-paced and ever-changing.

We're going to explore these myths in this book and identify new beliefs you need to embrace if you want to continue to perform at a high level, so that you don't get left behind, or, worse still, become irrelevant.

My passion for senior leaders knowing these myths, along with new beliefs I know to be true, stems from my certainty that to survive (and thrive!) in a rapidly changing world, which I liken to a vast, deep and at times treacherous ocean, it comes down to expert navigation.

However, this passion for helping others goes much deeper than this. While it stems from my navy days and developed during my years as a project manager and leadership coach, my enthusiasm also links directly to the satisfaction of seeing others achieve results that surpass their expectations. Their success becomes my elation when positive outcomes are achieved by competently manoeuvring away from 'old thinking.' Nothing gives me more joy than this.

By using this definitive 'compass' as a leader, you act as a valuable navigator in facilitating unparalleled business performance and results, which all stems from how you think. And the difference you can make goes well beyond what you can imagine.

This is a powerful guidance system that works—I've seen the difference that can be made to organisations, both big and small, in Australia and globally.

If this book resonates with you, and you seek the definitive 'compass' that will take your performance culture to a world-class level, then visit www.HighPerformanceCulturePartners.com.au/Consult to book a Complimentary Performance Strategy Session (value $795.00).

To your success,

Emma Sharrock
The Trusted Authority To Senior Executives On Creating High- Performance Cultures

CHAPTER 1

"The More Control I Have In My Organisation, The Better Results I Can Expect"

Picking up Charles Duhigg's book *Smarter, Faster, Better* was a revelation for me. One of the opening chapters describes a kidnapping case, which unfolded in 2014 and examines the role of control in decision making. It highlights how critical it is for leaders to rethink the role control plays, and how failure to do so not only erodes productivity and the bottom line but could cost lives.

My recollection of Duhigg's story goes something like this:

Having just returned from his usual Saturday morning bike ride, Frank Janssen, a 63-year-old national security consultant, couldn't help but smile. The sun was shining, there wasn't a cloud in the sky, and the neighbourhood kids were enjoying kicking their soccer ball back and forth. So, when he heard a knock at his front door, Frank didn't hesitate to answer.

The trio on Janssen's doorstep didn't look familiar. But the woman held a clipboard and was well-dressed, as were the two men, which led Frank to believe that they were possibly conducting a survey. So, he opened the door.

Without even an exchange of greetings, the two men barged through the front door, knocking Frank off his feet. While he struggled to comprehend what had just occurred, one of the men shoved a pistol in Frank's face, and the other pressed a stun-gun against his torso and pulled the trigger.

The voltage left Frank paralysed. The trio hurriedly cable-tied Frank's hands and feet before picking him up and throwing him in the boot of their silver Nissan. All three piled in the car, which slipped onto the freeway unnoticed.

Sometime later, Frank's wife returned home. Finding her front door ajar, blood on the porch and Frank's bike leaning against the shed without a sign of her husband sent her into a state of panic. She immediately contacted the police and disclosed that Frank had gone missing. Shortly after that, black FBI SUVs and police cruisers surrounded the Janssen home, and agents and officers began working together to tape off the property as a crime-scene, dusting for prints and collecting evidence.

What transpired over the next few days left Frank's wife's mind reeling. Stricken with concern over her husband's welfare, she found it difficult to concentrate on anything else; then the text messages started.

"We have your husband. He's in the boot of a car. And we'll send him back to you in boxes." These texts became more frequent and began to mention Janssen's daughter, an assistant district attorney, along with a man called Melton, who, according to police records, Janssen's daughter had helped to put away.

Subpoenaing evidence from the Melton case, which had seen the offender incarcerated for life, FBI agents turned to Sentinel, their evidence, clue and testimony management system. Linked to analytical engines and databases, Sentinel worked in conjunction with the Agile management process of pushing decision making to the people and teams closest to the problem.

The developer of Sentinel was a man named Fulgham, a former Wall-Street senior technical executive. He argued that the system would work only if bureau executives relinquished control and distributed critical decision-making capabilities to those in the field—the junior agents closest to the case. This approach also meant that FBI executives needed to shift away from traditional crime-fighting techniques and embrace flexible principles that would adapt to agent needs.

As Fulgham stressed, the FBI—like many other large organisations—planned everything around executives needing to approve every action.

Crime fighting, as with many other organisational problems, is unpredictable, with variables changing constantly. It's vital that decision making is shared, allowing agents at all levels to work autonomously. Waiting for approval is a bottleneck and slows progress. This could prove detrimental to the outcome, and in Janssens's case, his life.

Using Sentinel in the Janssen case, coupled with empowering junior agents to make critical decisions based on their field knowledge, the FBI rescued Janssen just before the involvement of boxes became necessary.

If You Don't Let Go, You Get Caught

I've witnessed first-hand how organisations get caught out by not letting go of control.

One case I recall as a stand-out: It was a close-knit business operation that appeared to be agile and flexible within their market but struggled to meet customer demands, despite their amazing work.

As it turns out, this company's founder, who the team perceived as having all the answers, had made it a requirement that he signed-off on absolutely everything. Every little decision made within the company, right down to the colour selection used in designs, needed the founder's permission before proceeding.

Now, while this doesn't sound unreasonable at first, the big problem here is that, in a day, there may be a handful or hundreds of decisions to make so that a project can move forward. If you're waiting for one person to sign-off on all these decisions, then the processes that lead to project completion become drawn out and extremely slow. The founder had inadvertently become a bottleneck.

Realistically, one person cannot always be available to make these needed decisions (in the case of the founder in this example, he wasn't). If you, as a leader, expect your team to wait for you to make and/or sign off on all the decisions, then you're not just delaying work but you're also reducing overall workplace efficiency, costing your organisation more to produce said work.

In turn, your client or clients start to become disgruntled due to deadlines not being met. This scenario becomes even more of a problem when the client needs a fast turnaround on the work.

Your employees are left twiddling their thumbs because you're not available to sign-off on decisions. Meanwhile the clock is ticking, and your client's deadline is blowing further out. Your client is not only under pressure to perform and reach key performance indicators but also must maintain their budgets and report to the board or their clients, who are also waiting. No one wins as everyone is caught in a negative spiral and ultimately damage control. Post incident reports may identify potential improvements in processes, specifically decision making, but they are rarely actioned as those improvements mean letting go of some control—which goes against everything you 'know to be true.'

Farmers in rural Africa, Asia and South America use this in-built resistance to let go of control to catch monkeys, which are considered pests.[1] The farmer sets a trap by filling a small vessel, usually a gourd, with nuts or treats that the monkey cannot resist. Then the farmer cuts a small hole in a termite mound and places the gourd inside.

The hole in the mound is just big enough for the monkey to fit their hand through. But not large enough for a monkey fist filled with treats. So, when the monkey grabs a handful of nuts, they become stuck.

The monkey wants the food badly and refuses to let go of it. However, as a result of holding onto the food, the monkey cannot get free. Instead, the monkey tries to get its full fist of treats out of the hole with no success, and this eventually leads to them being caught by the farmer.

The same applies to humans. We can be just like the monkey in that we don't like to let go. We simply must keep what's in our hand, and we truly believe we will achieve superior results if we're in control. Giving away control could lead to failure, and it's not worth risking the outcome, and ultimately our own self-worth.

Many leaders have this question: "If I am not controlling the situation, then what value am I adding to the organisation?"

The answer is: More than you could possibly know. The good news is there is a logical reason why that answer is difficult to appreciate. And it can be found by turning back the clock to the turn of the 20th century.

Moving From The Productionised Mindset To One Of Cultivation

Throughout the 1900s, one person having full control of any organisation was a part of daily work culture—it was the norm, along with every worker having a specific task that they completed before submitting for sign-off or approval. It was a factory-like process introduced to the world in the late 1800s by Fredrick Winslow Taylor, and came to be known as Taylorism.[2]

In its heyday, Taylorism was extremely successful. It led to an unprecedented scale of output for US factories just before World War II. It enabled organisations to accurately predict and control their workloads. The delegation of tasks flowed, and, once complete, the leader would sign-off on the task and then assign the next task.

The person responsible for sign-off was the leader/specialist, and they would have reached this senior position due to having that specialist knowledge.

Since then the world has changed. Our workplaces have become more demanding, complex and fast-paced. The factory-like process does not accommodate these new demands that call for not only more speed but flexibility and ability to adapt or 'pivot.' Waiting for sign-off hampers this ability significantly.

You're a key decision maker in your organisation, and it's likely that you've earned this level of respect. But, have you found that the numbers of key decisions are growing? Have you also found that the line of people waiting for approvals has also grown? Is work proceeding at a slower rate, and are there also far too many committees for your liking?

If you've answered 'yes' to any of these questions, then it's highly likely that you may be stuck in the past. You might not even be aware of this; however, the reality is that this approach may seem like it is mitigating risk and driving superior results, but it is slowing you and your organisation's rate of productivity down, which ultimately is costing you far more than you'd like to admit.

At one time, the command-and-control process of Taylorism was necessary. By controlling what the workforce did and separating tasks into repetitive units as part of a big machine, it enabled factories to get work done effectively by allowing for maximum efficiency.

The Cost Of Being In Control

But a problem started to arise when applying Taylorism to other types of work. Taylor's main belief was that money motivated all workers and they would work harder to receive their fair share.

This process works well for non-thinking, repetitive work; however, when you apply it to knowledge work, where thinking is required to solve problems—software engineering, accounting, pharmaceutical development, medical research and other thought-based work—then repetitive, controlled work impedes workers' ability to think and create. In your workplace this translates to employees not contributing and finding other ways to occupy their time. Employee feedback will describe a lack of motivation and feeling as though they're not a part of the 'big picture.'

In short, intelligent people don't respond well to controlled, repetitive work, as it makes them feel they are a part of the machine. Instead, they crave a motivating environment that stimulates their thought processes and empowers them to achieve results.

In an organisational-sense, when employees feel empowered like the junior agents in the Janssen case, they work harder, smarter and faster to deliver better results because they have decision-making authority to move forward at pace. Plus, these employees know that their leader and co-workers are equally committed to their success.

As a result, this further drives motivation with employees knowing that their innovation and insight will be highly regarded, rather than ignored, and that their team fully support their decisions.

If the junior agents in the Janssen case had not been empowered, and instead the control and decision making had rested with FBI executives, there would have no doubt been delays, which may have cost Janssen his life.

This story gives me chills. The people who kidnapped Janssen were on the verge of executing him when they were discovered. But, because the FBI executives delegated control to those who were closest to the case, the agents were able to move quickly, and Janssen was found before the fatal event transpired.

The Officer Of The Watch

It's uncanny, but most people think that the Navy is command-and-control driven, much like Taylorism. I can understand this because, on the surface, the Navy appears hierarchical-based—"Yes, sir" or "No, Ma'am," with specific ranks and seniority.

And yet, this is not the case at all. In fact, a warship could not function effectively (or at all) without empowered decision making. As the Officer of the Watch, it was my responsibility to make decisions that kept the ship and its crew safe. These decisions, especially time-critical ones, were often made without the captain's specific approval at the time.

The captain, like anyone else, needs to rest—it is impossible for him or her to be in command around-the-clock. So, when the captain retired for the night, they would leave what is known as "night orders."

These night orders were high-level guidance. There were no step-by-step instructions. Instead, they were guidelines that enabled me to use my initiative as the officer in charge throughout the night. I would only contact the captain in an event specified in night orders (for example, making landfall), or I felt that further guidance was required.

Taking on the responsibility of a ship while the captain slept taught me that it is not always the person most senior in the hierarchy who is the best person to make decisions all the time. Upon occasion, if that leader is absent (as when the captain of my warship was asleep) or they have no involvement in what is happening at the time (like the FBI leaders who weren't in the field in the Janssen case), then their judgement may be impeded. Plus, it may also take too long to get them up-to-speed, which in the case of a warship could cost lives, much like the FBI's Janssen case.

Traffic Lights Versus Roundabouts

Traffic lights and roundabouts are similar in that both manage traffic. But this is where the similarities end. Both are very different in HOW they manage traffic. The traffic light has absolute control, stopping and starting the traffic from a centralised position; whereas the roundabout's control is decentralised and able to adapt, so the traffic continues to flow.

Let's look at both in greater detail.

> Con-
> sider a roundabout com-
> pared to a set of traffic lights. The
> traffic lights have ulitimate control with
> traffic frequently stopping and starting, and
> drivers having no choice but to obey, lest they
> cause an accident. A roundabout on the other
> hand is dynamic, with decisions left to drivers,
> which means less regidity and more flow. A
> roundabout does not rely on a central
> decision making entity but rather a
> system of drivers working
> together.

The traffic light, which was invented in 1868 by a railway signalling engineer, adopted the three-colour light system in 1918.[3] Traffic lights control the decisions that vehicle drivers make on the road.

For instance, if the light is RED, you STOP. If the light is AMBER, you prepare to STOP. If the light is GREEN, you GO.

But, if you disobey the traffic light and you STOP when the light is GREEN, then you risk causing an accident. The same applies if you GO when the light is RED, since you may also cause an accident or risk prosecution for breaking the law.

The traffic light's sequence is also pre-determined, as is the length of the light staying one colour. The light does not adapt to its environment.

Roundabouts have been around since the 1900s but were only formalised in the UK in 1966 through the 'priority rule'. Modern roundabouts emerged in the US in the 1990s. Roundabouts (sometimes called traffic circles) create order by allowing the drivers of the vehicles to make decisions based on simple rules.[4]

The roundabout has no pre-determined point of control; instead, it allows the vehicle drivers to make decisions based on what is happening around them within their environment. This principle slows down traffic and allows it to flow continually, rather than to stop altogether.

While both the traffic light and the roundabout display control over traffic, the more traditional traffic light is not adaptable to its environment, whereas the roundabout is.

As a leader, executive or a business owner and manager, you want to move away from the rigidity of the traffic light and create roundabouts in the workplace.

'Traffic-light control' was definitely causing issues in an organisation I worked with recently. This group was exceptionally budget conscious, especially when it came to work-related travel, as it allowed them to maintain profitable outcomes by controlling costs. This focus on cost control meant that all travel required senior executive sign-off.

The problem was that this executive was not always in the office or available to sign-off travel requests. They frequently travelled themselves and were out of contact or were required in other locations.

Consequently, they were not able to approve all travel in time, which meant that employees missed workshops, conferences and other important meetings. Or, they were still able to make their commitments, but due to the late approval were stung with higher conference fees, air-fares and accommodation costs.

The irony of this is clear. The process (designed to control costs) actually saw the company lose out financially. Plus, in many instances, the missed workshops and meetings resulted in incomplete, sub-standard or delayed work, which, again, cost the company in terms of profitability.

Key Takeaway

- The more control you are happy to let go of, the more control you will have. But, to gain more control, you need to be prepared to shift your mindset away from your old way of thinking.

  "If you want real control, drop the illusion of control: let life live you."

  -- Byron Katie

CHAPTER 2

"I'm At My Best In Times Of Complete Certainty"

Walking through the park on a particularly windy day, I noticed a mother duck and her ducklings battling to stay upright on their webbed feet in the strong gusts. The mother duck led the way, and each duckling followed as they waddled across the grass in a line. In total there were 11 ducklings, all in perfect formation following one behind the other.

Watching the ducks, I was astounded when the wind blew the mother duck off her feet, and several of the ducklings rolled across the grass. All scrambled to their feet in mere seconds, shook themselves off, and then immediately started to reform the line behind their mother, who had barely paused before continuing to move.

The ducks then continued as if nothing had occurred. They didn't wait to be given instructions; instinctively they just did what they had to so that they gained momentum.

As the ducks waddled past, it occurred to me that the mother duck was the leader, like the executive of a business, and the ducklings her team members. Together, all collectively worked towards achieving the same goal. If this was the case, then the gust of wind could be viewed as an element of uncertainty that could prevent the team from reaching their objective.

The more I thought about it, I realised that as a leader or executive of any organisation that it was important to get moving, just like the ducks. Regardless of the project type, and even if all the contributing factors or specific tasks aren't set out, you must be okay with getting the project underway and giving it momentum. Otherwise the project may stall, which could derail the project, and possibly even your department or organisation.

How? You ask.

Highlighters & Project Certainty

Many executives and leaders want certainty. They need this factor in their organisation as it reassures them. I've witnessed this need first-hand on many occasions.

One such incidence occurred when I was working with a client to create a new product. The client was hesitant to move forward because there were many details of the project that they hadn't covered, and they didn't have all the answers.

I smiled at them when they said they needed greater project certainty before getting the project underway. Then I said, "That's like going into your study to find your highlighter." They looked at me puzzled. So, I explained.

Let's say you need a highlighter. You venture into your office to find it. You look in the top drawer of your desk and discover a mess. You know that your highlighter is in there somewhere, which encourages you to start rearranging the drawer in the hope of making it easier to find.

While rummaging through your drawer to find the highlighter, the idea of a drawer organiser pops into your head. So, you stop what you're doing, jump into your car and head off to officeworks to buy one.

While you're in officeworks, you notice the office furniture. It looks funky. You decide that your office is out-of-date and in desperate need of a freshen up.

When you finally get back to your office some hours later and eagerly begin unpacking your furniture, you notice that the carpet looks dirty. You then head off in search of the vacuum.

The scenario can go on and on, I explained to my client. And yet all this activity stemmed from the need to find a highlighter.

Sure, you've spent hours carrying out activities that supported your need to find the highlighter. But you never actually found the highlighter because you used your time elsewhere. When situations like this occur you need to stop and ask yourself, "What is more important? The highlighter or all of the supporting activity?"

My client nodded in response. Then he laughed. He appreciated that this was what he and his colleagues had done during their project meeting. They fixated on planning; many team members said they couldn't move forward because of this factor or that factor, which was the equivalent of them going in search of the highlighter and ending up at officeworks.

We later discovered that many of the factors the project team were concerned about became irrelevant. So, if the team had actually spent the hours developing these concepts and planning the project in its entirety, they would have wasted hours, possibly days and even weeks, needlessly.

Being Certain Of Safety & Security

But then you have to stop and ask yourself why you find it a necessity to plan everything down to the smallest detail before you can start the project. What's the compulsion for us to follow this type of behaviour?

It boils down to our need for certainty. We all like to feel safe and secure; it offers us a level of comfort. We may even perceive that we have certainty. But the reality is that we don't. When we relentlessly seek certainty we're not just missing out on opportunities, we're also putting ourselves at greater risk.

Let me explain.

When Cyclone Tracy hit Darwin in 1974 on Christmas Day more than 40 ships, including Navy vessels, prawn boats, ferries and schooners that sat in the safety of the harbour, were either damaged or destroyed.[1] However, the ships that went to sea were safe.

According to Navy reports, "Mountainous seas, whipped up by winds of 170 knots, were like crashing dumpers, and the harbour became strewn with wreakage."[2] Several naval vessels sunk in the safety of the harbour, while others, such as HMAS ADVANCE and ASSAIL, were safe after heading for open sea.

Thinking about these ships, you automatically assume that they are safer in the harbour. After all, they are near to land and help, if needed. Whereas those at sea appear more vulnerable and harder to get to should they need assistance.

And yet the ship that is in open water during a cyclone, or any storm for that matter, is safer, despite the uncertainty of the squall. This ship can manoeuvre, they can adapt, and they can outrun the storm. The ship in harbour is a sitting duck (as opposed to our moving ducks from earlier!), so to speak, lulled into a false sense of security, with no ability to change its plans, adapt, and ultimately survive.

The same applies to executives who perceive that they are at their best in times of complete certainty. They too are lulled into a false sense of security, with many believing that a detailed plan helps them to achieve this certainty that they seek. But, does it?

What may have worked in the past is no longer valid in this fast-moving world full of change and unpredictability.

Certainty is elusive, and those who wait may cost themselves far more than anticipated.

Turning back the hands of time gives us some insight into understanding this predicament further.

In the 90s, I worked on a number of IT projects. Back then, the pace of change was slower; certainty was an essential step that allowed teams to move forward with change. This certainty then helped project leaders and their teams determine strategic steps for the IT systems we were building.

These plans were also a must for the business, as without them an initiative would not be funded. As part of our planning, it was not unusual (in fact it was often compulsory) to create a detailed seven-year plan for data storage, right down to the number of users, the database requirements and anticipated storage capacity. Back then, storage was expensive, and those costs needed to be planned for. We were essentially trying to predict the future.

Today, the average IT system doesn't even last seven years.

Not only do today's systems last for less time but we also cannot be 100% sure if they will compete well in an already flooded market. Hence, we now build prototypes and test them early before we invest too much time, effort and resources into product creation. If we test the product as a prototype and it flops, then we can adapt the product until it meets the customer need, or we can scrap the idea completely and start again.

Given today's fast-paced world, new products and services are most often needed right now, rather than later. So, the team that pours its heart and soul into creating a foolproof plan in minute detail will find themselves missing the opportunity completely because another team elsewhere started with a simple plan and elaborated on it as they progressed.

Sure, the first team feel safer and more secure. But this sense of security is false because while they were feeling safe, the second team launched their prototype, tested the market, and were well on their way to having a viable product in the market.

Missing the opportunity is not the only problem the first team faces. This team may also encounter "Sunk Cost Bias,"[3] or the refusal to change, because they have invested all this time into detailed planning. This Bias occurs when teams have spent significant time on a product or project. There is an emotional attachment to the work done so far, even if it is only a plan. So, they press on, regardless of the cost.

Understanding Sunk Cost Bias

Pouring hours and hours into the development of products, services and investments, and collaborating to make ideas a reality, leads to emotional attachment. So, when we need to make changes to these decisions, we don't think rationally, and we find it difficult to alter or abandon what we've started. Thus, the "Sunk Cost" is our time and effort, and we've become biased because of this cost as we don't want to feel like we've wasted time developing these ideas.

Understanding the "Sunk Cost" becomes simplified when observing the game FarmVille.[4] This Facebook-based farming app, developed in 2009, attracted one in five users from the social media platform, or approximately 84 million users, in its heyday. However, by 2011, FarmVille's popularity dwindled to 50 million, and today it's estimated that around 1 million users frequent FarmVille23 daily. Now, while today's player figures sound dismal compared to the game's earlier days, you also must remember that we're talking eight years of gameplay here, which is colossal in an era and market that's super competitive with an estimated 500 new game apps launched daily.[5]

So, what's the attraction of FarmVille?

It's not played just for fun, if that's what you're thinking. No, FarmVille, for those of you who don't know, is investment-based in an emotional sense, and therefore it becomes addictive. Players invest so much time and effort into creating, developing and then nurturing their farm that the fear of loss generates Sunk Cost Bias. So they continue to play.

Now, if we turn our attention towards the nature of our decisions when we play FarmVille, or create a product or service plan when in business, we will see that all, regardless of complexity, involve uncertainty. We take a risk when decision making, whether this is calculated or spontaneous. But this is not all that happens.

Just before making any decision our brain thinks in terms of losses and gains.[6] We weigh up all situations and judge whether we stand to lose or succeed. So, when we combine these two elements—uncertainty and losses/ gains—our brain uses an automatic and often unconscious system to gauge whether we should proceed. After all, no-one likes to lose; it's instinctive. Therefore, the loss becomes a far more powerful motivator than the gain, with us trying to avoid the loss at any cost because loss hurts us emotionally.

Certainty's Cost

In a business sense, trying to avoid loss by following what you perceive as a certain plan or methodology towards success, can lead you down the wrong path. You not only miss opportunities because you're task-focused, but you also lack the needed flexibility to cater to the uncertainty that comes with making decisions. For instance, changing internal and external factors that alter a project's course, or those success-driven tasks that you have painstakingly worked hard to create.

I've witnessed this time and time again. Companies I work with spend so much time creating plans, rather than getting started. This approach is costly in terms of project timelines, plus it stretches resources and budgets.

A classic example of this is when I worked with a financial services organisation to implement an agile approach to project initiation. On average, it was taking six months for a business case to be approved so a project could start. I remember thinking at the time that this seemed like a long time, and it was.

The process involved a detailed business case document and many stakeholders contributing to it, mostly over email. As part of the change we introduced a collaborative approach to business case development. It involved face-to-face workshops focusing on the 'why' of a project and the high-level outputs the project team would produce.

Before we knew it, the six-month time-frame was transformed into six weeks. Our leaders were astonished. So much so, that they asked if we could apply this strategy more broadly across the organisation, beyond projects.

For me, reducing our project delivery time by 20 weeks was a monumental achievement, as collectively we had removed old and tired ways of thinking and their accompanying methodologies from the centre of the business world and packed them into a storage box. We had replaced them with a new way of thinking and a methodology to support this thinking. This had enabled the business to progress at a much faster rate, cutting costs and maximising the return on investment.

Implementing new strategies and shifting away from that old way of thinking is not easy. For many leaders, these older plan-driven strategies where you plan, plan, plan and then create an even more detailed plan are a proven way of working. But with the pace of change increasing rapidly, relying on this proven way of working from the past is a recipe for being left behind. And possibly made redundant, just like Kodak. Perhaps you know this story?

Kodak was the heavyweight in the photography ring, but in 2012 the giant declared bankruptcy after a century of dominance.[7] So, what went wrong?

Many believe that Kodak executives failed to see how the digital camera could make it in a world where film dominated. But this was not the case. A Kodak engineer invented the digital camera in 1975.[8] What led to the giant's failure was their fear of changing their marketing plan.

Kodak was so certain that their products marketed through 'Kodak Moments' were so powerful that their consumers would continue to use these regardless of technological innovation. So, they failed to cater to their consumer, believing that they too would be resistant to the change to digital.

Kodak's competitors, Sony and Canon, saw their chance and took it. Launching their digital cameras allowed them to steal a sizeable share of the market that Kodak had cornered. By the time Kodak realised they needed to get on board, their ship had sunk.

Looking at how Kodak's executives responded, we discover they were certain they would continue to dominate the photography market. And this certainty came from the marketing plan they had painstakingly developed that had dominated for four decades. This proven way of working meant the giant had enjoyed a 90% share of the US film market.

It can be easy to assume from this that the company operated at its best during these times of complete certainty. Unfortunately for them, this certainty vanished, and so did the company because it lacked flexibility and failed to adapt, or even see they needed to change, from their proven method of the past.

Change can seem awkward. You may feel as though you don't need it, and neither does your organisation. But, the truth of the matter is if you fail to plan for change, then you and the organisation you work for will experience a not so positive 'Kodak moment.'

Changing how you, as a leader, plan for change may seem like you're taking a leap of faith. But, are you?

The Illusion Of Taking A Leap Of Faith

We can all remember the Indiana Jones and the Temple of Doom movie and the scene where Indy takes that step across the chasm. Standing on the edge of the abyss, which appears bottomless, Indy's team calls out for him to help, "You must come quickly," they cry in desperation. Indy assesses the crossing: It's far too wide to jump, and if he makes a mistake then he won't survive the fall.

Instinctively Indy knows that there is more to this crossing than meets the eye. He whispers to himself, "It's a leap of faith" and then takes a step into what appears to be emptiness over the ravine.

The audience watching takes a deep breath. We expect Indy to fall or be left clinging for life on the side of the ravine. But he does neither of these. Instead, he appears to hover over the ravine, suspended in mid-air.

So, we ask as we watch the movie, "Is it a supernatural phenomenon? Why hasn't Indy fallen?"

Then the answer becomes clear as Indy looks around in total disbelief. He is standing on a narrow ledge that stretches across the chasm like a bridge from one side to the other. However, this ledge made of the same rock as the mountainous sides of the ravine that stretch up and down for hundreds, possibly thousands, of feet blends into the scenery, making it difficult to see.

Now you're wondering how Indiana Jones' actions relate to executive leadership?

Well, Indy's leap of faith is comparative for leaders because these executives need to take a step towards their goal regardless of the situation. By taking this step, leaders put their plan into action. Then as the plan unfolds, they learn more and gather momentum.

> Successful change is more like a series of small steps as a plan unfolds and iterates as we learn more. It may feel like a 'leap of faith' but rather it's a single step forward — one at a time.

By following this approach, a leader instinctively progresses and they continue to learn and direct effort towards the best possible outcomes. It's more of a process of progressing towards their goal, much like Indy who took the leap of faith.

Successful change is more like a series of small steps as a plan unfolds and iterates as we learn more. It may feel like a 'leap of faith' but rather one step forward at a time.

The leadership leap of faith is not hope-related but really about knowing that you're heading in the right direction. It's a little like starting a road trip from Melbourne to Sydney at night. You cannot see the exact path that you will travel from start to finish, but you have an idea of the roads that you will travel.

You jump in your car, turn your headlights on and start driving; you don't wait for the whole route in front of you to be visible. You don't need to see everything before you set off: just the road in front of you, illuminated by your headlights.

On your trip from Melbourne to Sydney you may encounter roadworks, traffic hazards such as kangaroos and other wildlife or even trucks carrying wide loads. All these obstacles will mean you may need to deviate off your original path. So you may need to adjust your initial plan.

The same applies to any plan. It too will need to adjust based on circumstances or what is happening in the ever-changing marketplace.

However, those leaders in search of complete certainty, because they feel this is when they work at their best, will need to plan their entire route of travel from Melbourne to Sydney right down to the last second. And, if they do this, they won't have time to make the actual trip.

A recent study I came across compounds this notion. The study, which focused on a company's adaptability, found that five-year plans mean very little these days.[9] The study surveyed over 1,350 chief executives in more than 75 countries and found that the biggest challenge faced by major companies were unknown events, with five factors— populism, migration, climate change, the fourth industrial revolution and an increase in short-term opportunism—eroding their capacity to plan.

Given this, many executives felt that in these uncertain times leaders needed to be courageous and embrace new ideas, new thinking and encourage innovation, especially when what we know to be true today could be irrelevant tomorrow.

In the world of business, waiting coupled with detailed planning equates to missed opportunities and decreased efficiency, which in turn reduces performance and erodes profit.

Key Takeaway

- You don't need to know everything before you take a step. Instead, you need to be willing to embrace ambiguity and move forward anyway.

  "In a storm, a ship is safest at sea, even in tumultuous waters, rather than in the harbour."

  -- Emma Sharrock

CHAPTER 3

"I'm Not Prepared To Trust Others Who Cannot Prove To Me That They Are Trustworthy First"

The Guggenheim Museum in Bilbao, Spain, is majestic and breathtaking, with titanium-cladding and flowing curves that leave you marvelling at its architectural beauty. Resembling a futuristic battleship complete with turret, the Museum appears moored in the Nervon River.[1]

This architectural feat is an annual draw-card that attracts thousands yearly, especially as the building changes colour in different lights. But it is not just the magnificence of this masterpiece that makes it enigmatic. It is also the fact that Frank Gehry, the designer of the Guggenheim, brought together many concepts, some tried and tested and others new and exploratory, and he also had the nouse to trust in others so that his original concept flourished and grew to become iconic and the saviour of a dying industrial region.

Let me describe how Frank Gehry pulled off this incredible feat.

Started in 1991, and completed in 1997, the Guggenheim is the work of pure genius. While Frank Gehry designed the original Guggenheim concept, he also knew that he could not single-handedly pull off such a monumental project. Instead, Frank Gehry enlisted the help of others. He welcomed their input, which allowed the project to develop and become so profound.

Wanting to replicate motion, Frank Gehry, who claimed to be computer-illiterate, used advanced Computer-Aided Three-Dimensional Modelling Interactive Application (CATIA) software, with the help of others, to design the museum.[2] All up, more than 150 team members collaborated to make the museum a success. More than 16,000 faxes sent during the project, along with countless daily phone calls and in-person six-weekly meetings, enabled everyone working on the project to share ideas.[3]

One such idea that transformed the museum was its façade. Having worked with metal facades prior to this project, the Guggenheim team didn't want the museum to appear too reflective on sunny days, or too grey and dull on overcast days. To find the right product for the façade the team nailed samples to a pole in the parking lot; when the titanium turned golden in poor light, they knew they had found their match.

Titanium, however, was twice the cost of other steel products and with the museum needing just under 43,000 panels, cost became a major consideration. Researching titanium properties, the team discovered that this metal was far stronger than steel, which meant that the panels could be thinner. The team also found a Russian company that had a glut of titanium, further decreasing prices. These factors saw titanium become the Guggenheim façade of choice.

Another challenge the team faced was putting the titanium panels in place. The sheer height of the museum required a crane, but cranes could not negotiate the curves of the building.

Many on the Guggenheim team claimed that high-tech and complex installation methods would be required, but after putting their heads together, they found a much simpler way to install the panels: training mountain climbers as installers. This strategy paid off, and just three years after completion the Guggenheim Museum made a profit, resurrecting Bilbao's economy and turning the city into a world-renowned landmark.

If we look critically at the success of the Guggenheim Museum, it becomes clear that it hinged on trust. Frank Gehry trusted 150 people to work with him to bring his ideas to life. Without the input of each person on the project, it is doubtful it would have come to fruition.

How does trust and the Guggenheim Museum relate to you and your team?

Needing Proof

I've encountered trust, or should I say the lack of it, in many organisations. A lack of organisational trust occurs in many ways, but most hinge on the need for proof.

For example, many senior executives want to see exactly how a solution will work before they put a specific strategy into action. In most cases, the evidence these executives seek needs to be data-orientated.

Figures talk volumes as these relate directly to the profitability of a project. But too much data slows down a project's progress as it's time-consuming to gather and it also stifles creativity, with the project becoming tedious and needlessly drawn-out. And often an opportunity is missed due to the time delays that result.

Thus, providing proof to establish trust before putting the solution into place is not always practical.

Another situation that typically is proof-orientated occurs when a leader and their team start work on a project. The leader may have worked with this team before, or the team may be a completely new group of people. The leader may have even hired experts to help them achieve their outcomes.

But, when a leader doesn't know these experts or their capabilities, they often don't trust in their abilities until they've seen these in action. Alternatively, they may have worked with a person or people prior on another project, but this project may require different skills, ones that they've not witnessed in action prior, which makes them want to see this ability once again.

Leadership Distrust

It's not personal. Often the team leader's distrust stems from being let down previously. They may have worked on other projects that have not come to fruition due to lack of skills. Therefore, the leader views this as having been let down, with team members not delivering what they should have delivered. But, if we look at these projects in more detail, the issues are usually handed down from the leader.

For example, let's say a team get together to work on improving customer retention. The leader hires several experts to help make this project a success. However, instead of letting these clever people get on with what they do best, the leader does not trust them, and the new team members feel as though they need to prove they are trustworthy.

As a result, the team leader disempowers the experts and other members of the team by taking the approach of handing out tasks for them to complete. The team respect the team leader, so they carry out these tasks.

Over time the experts and other team members lose interest in the project. Any ideas they had to improve the outcomes of the project have faded just like their enthusiasm.

The team then come to rely on the team leader's issued tasks and orders.

So, when the leader is absent, the team often don't know what to do. Consequently, progress on the project not only slows to a snail's pace but it fails to reach its fullest potential.

In some situations, the leader's behaviour can lead to intelligent people no longer being able to think for themselves. Why? Well, they've been given orders for so long that they've forgotten how to think for themselves.

Metaphorical Yum-Cha

One example of intelligent people forgetting how to think derives from a regular get together with friends. This group of pals meet for Yum-Cha at the same restaurant on the second Wednesday of each month.

One of the friends is especially passionate and knowledgeable about Yum-Cha. She also knows her friends and what they like and dislike. So, when the trolley arrives at their table, she orders for the table and delicious food materialises.

The friends have enjoyed Yum-Cha this way for years. Then, one day, the friend who does the ordering for the group is absent. The group arrive at the restaurant and are seated. But, when the waitress comes around to take their order, they are lost for words. The friend who usually places the order is not there, and it dawns on the group that they have no idea what to order without her guidance.

While this example centres on a group of friends, we can also look at the group as an organisation, with a leader and team members. The leader is the Yum-Cha aficionado friend, and the team members are the other friends in the group. When the leader takes a task-based approach, it only becomes apparent when the leader is absent that these intelligent team members are unable to think for themselves.

Adopting New Ways

In my Navy days, I witnessed the opposite. During an emergency such as a man overboard, as the Officer of the Watch I would often call out orders to my team members.

At the time of any emergency, the ship is chaotic. And yet everyone knows their roles as they are well-practised due to their knowledge and the many drills we carry out. They know exactly what needs to be done.

The process unfolds smoothly, with my called-out orders only serving to confirm the activities that need to be done rather than as a delegation. In many cases, the team may carry out an activity well before an order is given. After all, if you have seen a person fall into the water, you don't wait to be told to push a lifebuoy overboard.

During such situations, the captain trusted me as the Officer of the Watch to make decisions in the moment, like turning the ship in the best direction to recover a man overboard. Practice drills were the time to experiment and learn. If I suggested a different solution, he would consider it and most likely say, "Let's give it go." Never did he ask for detailed evidence as to the why and what of the solution.

Having seen trust instilled in Navy staff without first needing detailed proof of their trustworthiness, I know that this methodology works firsthand. However, for senior executives who have not used this trust-based approach in the past successfully, adopting a new way is not that easy.

The Journey Of Specialist To Generalist

When you work in an organisation for several years, you become a specialist in your field. Over time you get to know how a segment of the organisation works, and you know this extremely well. You have faith in your expertise, and you trust your instincts in this role.

As time progresses, you get promoted. Your role changes. Your perspective shifts. Your once-simple role becomes more complex. You also find that your specialist knowledge needs to become more generalist as you now span wider vistas and scaling your specialist knowledge in all these new areas is not possible.

Becoming a generalist has also made you doubtful of your ability to cope in this new context, which, in turn, erodes your trust in your own ability to perform. For some leaders, this leads to putting on a tough, professional exterior and adopting the 'fake it until I make it' approach.

But the reality is this exterior is transparent, and many people, including your team members, can see through this front. So, while it can sometimes feel demoralising to encounter challenges and not cope as well as you feel you should, it also exposes your vulnerability and allows others to see that you are not able to do all tasks equally as well.

Having experienced this firsthand as a leader myself, I know that I felt the need to show my team how devoted I was to my role. As a result, I would come into the office early, and I would always leave late to stay on top of all aspects of my role.

Sure, my work was always up-to-date, and I was often ahead in tasks, but I also projected a superhuman image made of unobtanium. This image displayed no vulnerability and indicated to my team that I didn't trust in their abilities to do their work adequately. Fortunately for me, my team gave me this feedback, and I was able to take action to show that I did trust them, and that I too didn't always have all the answers.

Years ago, I also worked with a CEO who once was this specialist. He had detailed, specific knowledge, and yet when he became CEO, he found he was unable to practise and demonstrate this knowledge within his leadership team. It was a sizeable challenge for him to come to terms with this change, but by understanding that he couldn't do the detailed work he once knew and loved, he also grasped that he was able to lead without being in the detail and tasking others.

He had to establish trust in the abilities of his team to carry out their roles well, and in some cases better than he could due to being more up to date and close to the knowledge. If he didn't trust his team, then the result would be a loss of productivity that would eventually erode the business profitability.

Another CEO that I worked with faced a similar challenge. This CEO needed to get a new product out, and, at the same time, they also had to meet the expectations of several recent regulatory changes. These changes affected the launch of the new product so extensively there was a risk of it being rendered worthless.

As a specialist in the area the product catered to, the CEO found it difficult not to manage the product redevelopment and delegate the team tasks. But, knowing that this technique would slow down the product revision, and possible launch, the CEO called a crisis meeting with his team to resolve the problem.

With both the CEO and the team under extreme pressure to turn around the product so that it didn't become obsolete, the CEO presented the problem of the new regulatory changes to the team and facilitated a discussion to come up with ideas to move forward. The team faced with this dilemma knew that they had to be both resourceful and swift to overcome the regulatory changes and enable the product to reach its fullest potential.

The resulting product suited the market and its needs and adhered to the regulatory changes. It was also nothing like the CEO had imagined. Trusting the skills of the team exceeded all expectations.

If, however, the CEO had chosen to take control and make the needed changes to the product based on his own skills and experience, then it is highly unlikely the result would have been as successful. In fact, considering the currency of the CEO's knowledge in this area, the result would have been a failure.

To put this concept of adapting to change into perspective, let's look at the human body and how it reacts to change that could be detrimental to the system, in an organisational sense.

The Human Body Organisation

Think about cutting your finger. When you cut your finger, your body reacts automatically to repair the cut so that the wound is closed, and you avoid infection. To do this, the human body needs to undertake a series of processes that involve several types of cells going into immediate action.

Each of these cells has a role to play in repairing the wound. However, they go about their work automatically; they don't wait for instructions on what to do.

The first group of cells cleans the wound site and captures any invaders. The next group starts to rebuild the wound, replacing tissue and broken blood vessels. The third group closes the wound, and the fourth spreads collagen around to strengthen the site, increase its durability and reduce scarring.[4]

So, if we look at this scenario from an organisational perspective, we can see that each of these groups of cells is a team member in a larger group, which in this case is the human body. The response by the body comes from the central nervous system, which is orchestrated by the brain. So, in this respect, the brain can be viewed as the senior executive or team leader.

While the brain gives the initial command to start the project of repairing the wound, it does not delegate individual tasks to each cell individually. Instead, these cells automatically respond as a part of a larger system. Therefore, each part of the human body trusts that the other part can carry out its role adequately so that collectively they can repair the wound and prevent infection.

The repair of a wound on the human body must happen fast. If the cells take too long, then infection can compromise the whole system. The same applies to an organisation, with the cost of taking too long to establish trust presenting in many forms—from lost opportunities to complete irrelevance.

The Cost Of Establishing Trust

Organisations encounter problems when they are working on anything that involves changing the status quo. Variables occur, and these need to be overcome to keep the change moving forward smoothly and in line with anticipated deadlines.

When we look back in history, we can find many examples of project failure. Reports indicate that in the U.S alone more than $250 billion is spent annually on IT projects that fail, with the average cost of each project's development between $430,000 and $2.3 million. Plus, more than 31% of projects stall before they've even started, and over 50% of projects cost more than 180% of their original targeted cost.[5]

Denver International Airport is an example of the cost of trust. The airport project team failed to produce baggage handling software over the course of a project that extended throughout the 1990s. The system was scrapped in 2005 and replaced with a fully manual system, with maintenance costs reportedly running at $1 million a month at the time.

In a 'post mortem' on the fiasco, one of the consistent themes was the failure of the project executive team to recognise the complexity of the project. Specialists had identified a number of potential issues that meant the project would take longer than the anticipated two years.

The executive team did not listen and ploughed on regardless. If they had listened to the specialists, and trusted their assessments, this story may not have had the unfortunate end that it did.

The difference between successful projects like the Guggenheim Museum and failures like the Denver Airport baggage handling system is the team's ability to trust in the judgement of the experts working on the project. Exhibiting this trust during times when the project flows smoothly leads to even greater trust when problems do arise. This trust also elevates a team's confidence so that they work even harder to find a solution.

Plus, projects that fail like Denver Airport's baggage handling software often have unrealistic expectations and don't give their team members enough space to fully develop their ideas, especially in terms of time constraints. In turn, these projects cannot adapt when issues are identified.

Often when on manoeuvres in the Navy, timing was imperative to the success of our missions. Delays could jeopardise our ability to successfully complete them.

However, if a critical issue was identified, such as a risk to an engine or electrical system, the captain listened and trusted in his experts, even if the identified risk meant a delay and ultimately failing to achieve a mission objective. This trust was not based on a detailed knowledge of the ship's engineering components, but rather on the abilities of the team.

This leads to another factor that contributes to a lack of trust for many senior executives. They may have started in an organisation back in their younger career days and worked their way up from there.

Over these years of practice, in an era far slower paced than today, these executives came to rely on the 'proven' approach of suggesting a solution and then testing it so adequate data could substantiate its viability. However, in today's fast-paced world, waiting for this evidence is no longer possible if an organisation wants to maintain productivity and market position.

The Speed Of Trust

Lack of trust in business effects not only profits, but it also erodes reputation. The business that can establish trust fast reduces their costs and increases the efficiency and production of their teams and organisation.[6] Not having trust in team members or feeling that you need to establish trust as a leader leads to defensive behaviour, which further erodes relationships and, ultimately, results.

Research suggests that projects often fail because organisations place more emphasis on project factors than on team member engagement. These costs are often financial, erode team member confidence and can compromise the integrity of an organisation and expose it to greater threats such as security breaches.[7]

But often trust comes from within. It is not so much our need to establish trust in others, but our need to trust ourselves that increases organisational trust. By examining how we behave—our habits, how we react, our thought processes—we can uncover a great deal about ourselves. It is, therefore, this examination of oneself which establishes the speed of trust.

The Guggen-
heim Museum in Bilbao is a stunning example of craftmanship and trust
that resulted in an outcome far greater
than the sum of individual parts. By providing a vision and the trust in skilled
craftspeople to bring it to life,
Frank Gehry created
something truly
profound.

The speed of trust is the rate of trust establishment and the speed of project completion. Trust is not just emotion-based; it is finding a middle ground or level of comfort that is based on reason and thought that is without suspicion. When you exhibit suspicion and distrust, others see this as further disempowering the team and eroding productivity.

Frank Gehry epitomised the speed of trust when he developed the Guggenheim Museum. He had a vision, and by trusting in others and their skills, he enabled this vision to develop, with the result being far greater than the sum of the parts that contributed to Guggenheim's initiation.

Understanding what trust is and how it contributes to projects within an organisation enables you as a leader to realise your full potential. Plus, it gives team members the opportunity to feel that they are a valuable resource, with their input having a positive impact on a project's outcome.

Key Takeaways

- Give trust freely. Empower your teams.

  When you do, you will be amazed at what your people will achieve. They will also trust you back.

- Also, remember that you need to trust yourself to give trust and that the reward is high performance.

  Ask yourself, "How much do I trust myself?" Answer honestly and you'll reap the reward.

"… Many things have a plurality of parts and are not merely a complete aggregate but instead some kind of a whole beyond its parts…"

-- Aristotle

CHAPTER 4

"I Work Better In A Spontaneous Manner As Structure Around Me Suppresses My Potential"

US Navy Seals are known as the elites of combat. They serve to protect their nation, and they do so in a very disciplined fashion. And this discipline gives them a lot of freedom. While this sounds almost contradictory, it's worth taking a sneak peek at how a US Navy Seal starts their day to understand the context.

A Navy Seal lies sleeping. Beside his bed there are three alarm clocks lined-up. The first alarm is electric; alarm two is battery powered; and three is a good-old-fashioned windup. These three clocks ensure that there are no excuses for not getting up in the morning.[1]

When the alarms go off, discipline begins for the Seal. This routine is the first test for the day, one that sets the tone for what will follow. The Seal has two choices: He can get out of bed the moment the alarm sounds, which means he passes the test, or he can stay in bed in the comfort and warmth and display his weakness.

While the act of getting out of bed is simple and it seems almost insignificant, it holds far more power than many people realise. When you're disciplined, you reap the rewards constantly. Getting up earlier gives you more free time. Training your body to become physically stronger means you move easier and with more fluidity. Eating a balanced, well-maintained diet free of preserved foods increases your health and your vitality. All these aspects lead to a happier, more fulfilling life filled with freedom.

This same freedom is achievable as a leader because discipline demands control, and the more structured you are, the greater your potential.

So how is it that so many leaders of organisations prefer spontaneity, which allows them to express themselves more freely?

This thinking comes from an aversion to frameworks and structured approaches. Many leaders have experienced management frameworks with little flexibility— structures which haven't worked well for them due to the need to 'follow to the letter' and the subsequent stifling of creativity.

Many leaders use a 'copy and paste' approach, rather than trying to understand the intent of the framework and applying it to suit their purpose. Many fail to work out a framework's purpose, or their working environment's culture, so that they can apply the framework in a way that gets results. Spotify is an excellent example of applying a framework purposefully to shift an organisation's culture.

Started in 2011 in Sweden, Spotify is a music streaming technology that has been highly successful. So, naturally, others see this success and want to follow in this group's footsteps: They appear to have all the answers, as well as having found a model that works where others have failed.

Spotify, on the other hand, stresses that their model (which they vehemently restate is not a model at all) won't work for others as it derives from Swedish culture. A culture, says Spotify, which is very different from that in, say, the United States or England.

Thus, applying this framework directly to another company in another country and culture is not going to work. It's a little like Starbucks, the American coffee giant, opening in Australia and trying to apply their framework to the existing Australian coffee culture. The result wasn't pretty.[2]

Starbucks has locations all over the world; its stores are in more than 28,000 locations, in over 76 countries. But, while it's successful in other countries—a new Starbucks opens every 15 minutes in China—Starbucks cannot nail the Australian market. Company losses in Australia at one point totalled more than $105 million.[3]

Looking at why this failure occurred, many suggest that Starbucks, like many other successful businesses, applied the same business model in a very different environment. What Starbucks leaders failed to understand is that this new environment was not the same as previous environments— the people were different, the culture was different, and the model needed to be adapted to work. Failing to adapt the framework in response to a different enviornment set the business up for failure.

These 'framework failures' have prompted leaders to look towards a more spontaneous or organised approach as they perceive that this will fit their needs better; they'll stimulate their team, drive motivation and create an emotional connection. Plus, they'll generate sustainable success. But, will they?

Stimulation, Motivation And The Emotional Connection

Stimulating, motivating and creating an emotional connection is what Sir Richard Branson and others known as influencers do so well; they drive branding by giving products and services personality. This ability turns what seems to be lacklustre into something shiny and alluring, so we want to know more. Ultimately, such results act as a draw-card because we see success. But we don't always see the full picture. We only see what we want to see.

The perfect example of this is a business facilitator who graced the business mentorship arena years ago. This facilitator worked any room like magic, captivating a group's attention in an instant with a charismatic approach. He transformed boring into an adventure and sent a wrecking-ball through dull.

The people who worked with this facilitator couldn't get over how effortless his approach appeared. He breezed into a workshop five minutes before it started, coffee in hand, and he'd say, "Hi everyone, let's get started." Then the workshop would begin without so much as a hiccup, the whole room captivated by this facilitator's every move.

So powerful was this facilitator's approach that many who attended his workshops wanted to emulate him. A number even tried his approach. They would arrive just before a workshop, coffee in hand, trying to turn on their charismatic, magical and spontaneous approach. However, it didn't work. They appeared awkward, disjointed and unprepared. Their workshops achieved nothing, and they felt like they had failed. But had no idea why.

What those who tried to emulate the facilitator failed to see at first glance was that he had decades of experience. He had built strong relationships with many people, which allowed him to stroll into a room and feel comfortable owning that space. Plus, he adapted his approach to suit the situation; underneath the spontaneity was a strong structure.

So why is this so prevalent in business?

We all think we want spontaneity in our life. It appears to give us more freedom. Many aspire to be as interesting and charismatic as people like Sir Richard Branson who appear to be kitesurfing and hot air ballooning every moment they can. These acts are spontaneous and fun, aren't they? Or, are we only looking at the surface and not at what lies underneath?

Sir Richard Branson: Spontaneous Or Structured?

Touted as "the most interesting man in the world," Sir Richard Branson seems spontaneous and carefree. He owns an island and more than 400 companies across the globe. Sir Richard is also renowned for his outlandish PR stunts—flying around the world in a hot air balloon, wearing a wedding dress, driving a tank in New York City, dressing as a flight attendant and jumping off the roof of a Las Vegas casino.[4] All acts appear spontaneous and incredibly fun.

Wearing denim jeans to work and loathing ties, along with anything related to 'stuffy corporate culture,' Sir Richard Branson seems extremely spontaneous. However, if we look closer, nothing he does is spur-of-the-moment. His daily life is extremely structured, and this helps him to not only finish what he started but to achieve great things, by making the most of every hour.

Waking up at 5am every day, Sir Richard Branson prefers to jump out of bed and exercise—tennis, walking, running, biking or windsurfing are just some of his favourites. He then eats breakfast and takes the time to enjoy his family because this sets the mood for the day and gets him in the right mindset for business.[5]

His first port of call once in his office are his emails. He also likes to be online early so this makes him accessible and engaged. Plus, it connects him to his offices, and as he says, "allows him to have his finger on the pulse."

Between emails and calls, Sir Richard catches up on the news and blogs. Then, he shares his writing with the word via social media—Facebook, Twitter, LinkedIn and Instagram.

Other daily rituals for Sir Richard include drinking copious amounts of tea throughout the day and carrying a notebook wherever he goes. This secret, he says, is his "life hack" as it allows him to write down all his thoughts as they come to him, wherever that may be.

Having a structured life and approach to business, however, is not how we initially perceive him. Instead, we view Sir Richard Branson and other celebrities and role models how we want them to appear. We see their success, and we want to apply this to our own lives.

But the reality is what's on the surface is not how these people that we admire live their life. Instead, they are very disciplined and structured, and this is what enables them to reach the heights that they do.

If we had the same discipline, the same structure, would our lives be the same as our role models'?

No, because like Spotify and Starbucks, we would need to adapt each structure and discipline to suit our purpose. It is doable, and not made of unobtanium. But we must think about our purpose. This thinking then gives us the ability to move beyond the belief that spontaneity leads to freedom.

So, if we don't follow a specific business structure and adopt a more spontaneous approach what happens?

The Cost Of Spontaneity

Having worked with clients who pride themselves on having a culture based on spontaneity, where they actively resist any framework as this stifles their creativity, it becomes apparent that they are not reaching their fullest potential. Instead, they lose their hold on their market share. Let's look at an example.

One company that started from the ground up began with a small number of people. The best approach for them at the time was spontaneity; it worked well for them. A quick conversation across the desk could move them in a new direction quickly, which resulted in them dominating a growing market.

However, as the company gained ground, more people were needed to keep up with demands. The spontaneity that had contributed to their fast success was now creating chaos—poor customer support, a lack of continuity, and inadequate performance—which led to the company losing their market share.

Slipping from being number one in their market to number three was a reality check for this company. They opened their eyes to other possibilities and sought out help to implement change.

After discussing options, they opted to try a framework that fitted their purpose. Although the discipline initially felt like it was slowing them down, over time they found that this framework gave them the freedom to pursue their creativity. Plus, it enabled them to regain their lost market share.

However, if this company had failed to alter their structure to meet the demands of the marketplace, then it is highly likely they would have continued to lose market share. As a result, this company would have joined Starbucks and a long list of business failures in Australia.

Keeping Structure Simple

It is also vital that as a business you don't make your structure too complicated. Over complicating structure makes simple tasks difficult and extremely time-consuming. So, what should have taken minutes, now takes hours. Such complication reduces productivity in business, and this erodes profitability. Complicated business structures also lead to role confusion, procedural issues, and a lack of coherence.

Some of Australia's most successful businesses have simple structures. Many of these structures are based on frameworks founded on the trust and respect of the employees and the customer—without which any business will fail to deliver.

For example, the Australian company Atlassian is famous for its five values that guide "what we do, why we create, and who we hire." These values are printed on the t-shirts that the staff happily wear. While this appears to be a novel concept, this visibility unifies the team; all staff know what's expected of them, and the customers know what to expect of the company.

Thus, a framework that's connected to purpose, easily followed and interpreted by all within the business, leads to success. It's a little like thinking of a business's structure like we do an AFL (Australian Football League) game. In an AFL game, there's a field with lines marked around the perimeter, and goal posts. To score you must kick the ball through these goals. These aspects of the game are all pre-determined. So, they represent a framework or structure that needs to be followed to be successful or to win the game. If you don't follow the game rules, then you'll be penalised, which can lead to your team losing the match.

By following this framework all AFL players understand the rules; they know what expectations others have of them, and how they can be successful. These rules give all players a clear direction; they know what they must do to achieve success. But, once the initial ball is bounced anything can happen, so they also use their skills and creativity to achieve results; they run fast, change direction and jump higher, all so they can win the match, be successful and claim victory.

If we compare an AFL game to a business, we discover that they have a great deal in common. The AFL game has structure, as does a successful business. Both have rules in place that enable them to achieve results. All players know these rules, and while they follow them, they can also use their creativity to increase the impact that these rules have, which in a business sense means the staff can go out of their way to help customers, make the experience more memorable, and connect on a higher level. These aspects take an ordinary encounter with a business and make it extraordinary, one that a customer remembers and shares with others; it creates an illusion of magic.

Mastering Business Magic

The Australian-born son of Vietnamese refugees, Vinh Giang (a former accounting student) created the *Encyclopaedia of Magic*, which teaches others how to orchestrate magic in their life. Using magic metaphorically Vinh Giang breaks through illusions, he helps to problem-solve and teaches others how to use the power of perspective.[6]

Any-

t h i n g

unfamiliar can look chaotic. In one of his presenta-

tions, Vinh Giang invites us to consider an image of random

shapes. We simply cannot make sense of it. Until we suddenly

can. And this new understanding can come from another

perspective, such as a fresh set of eyes. You can never look at

that original image the same way again. You too can see

order in the

chaos.

So, how does magic relate to business?

In a rapidly changing world where marketing contantly bombards us, and new products and services get introduced every second, it's getting hard to rise above the ordinary.

Magic creates an illusion, one that is awe-inspiring, just like Sir Richard Branson and other influencers who weave their magic. What is magic? According to Giang, it's simply 'a problem you cannot solve.'

To break free of norms we need to take a different perspective. We do that, and we create awe.

Key Takeaway

- With discipline comes freedom. The mindset shift is a 'fit for purpose framework' that sets the scene and allows for emergent, creative behaviours.

  "Discipline equals freedom and allows for creative possibilities to emerge."

  -- Jocko Willink

CHAPTER 5

"I Believe Complex Problems Require A Complex Solution"

Having negotiated turbulent seas and foul weather, a Naval warship on routine manoeuvres found itself engulfed in a thick fog. Concerned about the lack of visibility, the captain stayed on the bridge to keep an eye on the crew's activities.

As the night progressed, the fog density increased and visibility became strained with the crew finding it difficult to see past the end of the bow. The captain grew more tense.

A short time later the lookout on the bridge called out, "Captain! A light, bearing on the starboard bow."

Concerned as to the proximity of the light to the warship, the captain asked, "Is it moving or steady?"

The lookout responded that it was steady. This announcement signified that the warship was on a dangerous collision course with the other vessel.

The captain immediately ordered his signalman to relay a message to the other vessel, "We're on a collision course. I advise that you alter your course to 20 degrees east."

With a quick comeback, the other vessel replied, "You change your course 20 degrees west."

Agitated by the arrogance of the reply, the captain ordered his signalman to respond with, "I am a captain. You change your course 20 degrees east."

Back came the reply, "I am a second-class seaman, you had better change your course 20 degrees west."

This response infuriated the captain. "How impertinent!" he thought. He shouted at his signalman to send back a message that read, "I am a warship. Change course 20 degrees east immediately."

Back came an almost instant answer, "I am a lighthouse. Your call."

This renowned urban legend, which first began in the mid-1930s, relates to the belief that a complex problem needs a complex solution.[1] The problem, a possible collision between two vessels, seems to need a complex solution that depends on movement from another party. However, had the captain of the warship simply altered course, as first suggested, then time and resources would not have been wasted, and the risk of collision reduced.

So, how do we as leaders have a tendency to seek out a complex solution for a complex problem?

I was coaching an IT team who had just come together to work on a project, and they were trying to work out how they could advise another team that they had finished their portion of the work. After about 15-minutes of discussion that involved creating everything from apps through to the use of post-it-notes, one the team members, an 18-year-old, said, "Why don't we just talk to each other?"

Everyone in the room just stopped and stared. It was so quiet in that room as the team contemplated the suggestion. A suggestion, mind you, that involved no more effort than walking across a small office space. They all agreed it was a great idea—simple and effective with little use of resources.

Wasting Time & Other Valuable Resources

When a complex problem presents itself, leaders immediately seek out a complex solution. But, when they elect to go down this path, the complex solution tends to waste valuable time, effort and money.

Trying to solve a complex problem with a complex solution has surfaced time and again within mostly large organisations. In most cases, the automatic reaction of leaders is to call on the help of a specialist to resolve the issue. But sometimes this specialist isn't necessarily required as an easy fix can resolve the problem.

A perfect example of this was a security program I worked on several years ago. With a number of teams responsible for different aspects of the project, we needed to touch base to ensure the program flowed smoothly and delivered its promised results.

Several weeks into the initiative, the program director wanted all project leaders to meet so they could share their progress with each other. This meeting was critical to the program's completion as all teams were interconnected and relied on one another to complete their work within some tight timeframes.

In preparation for the meeting, the program director asked each project leader to prepare a 15-minute presentation which summarised the team's work on their aspect of the program. This presentation needed to briefly define the project, its scope and any potential risks, as well as include recommendations for overcoming those risks.

The sheer complexity of the work and the interconnecting parts between the teams made it difficult to condense the information into a 15-minute presentation. But, not impossible. So, several leaders took the time to prepare a short yet informative update about their section of the project. They even took the time to rehearse their updates with each other to get early feedback and ensure they met the time limitation.

On the day of the presentations, we all took a seat. Several leaders presented their team summation, and they were short and to the point. This methodology made it easy to understand their aspect of the project and how they were managing risks and complexity.

I was looking forward to the opportunity to present my team's work and share how we had dealt with some complex problems and was still on target to meet deadlines. However, one more project leader stood between me and this opportunity. This project leader stood up and started to make her presentation. From the start it was clear she had not prepared, as she seemed to meander through a range of points.

An hour and three quarters later no-one in the room had any idea what her team were working on, let alone how they were tracking against timeframes. Knowing that there were others in the room, including myself, who still needed to present their project, I asked if she was almost finished.

In response, this person said, "This is a very complex project that requires a complex presentation." And yet many of us agreed that her team's side of the project wasn't that complex. Although by making it appear more difficult than it was she was able to justify her need for a complex explanation and give her project greater significance.

Other examples of the need for leaders to find complex solutions for complex projects present when examining government initiatives. For instance, a Queensland Government IT project where court results were to be delivered electronically had an estimated budget of $550,150 with a 12-month completion. However, the project encountered difficulties in terms of technical risks; so specialist contractors were hired to identify these complex risks, which resulted in delays of over 12 months and a budget blow-out of $785,000.[2]

Another government example of a complex project problem needing a complex solution is the new ASIO headquarters in Canberra. Defined as the crown jewel of the Australian intelligence community, ASIO's head office has blown out its budget on several occasions.

The first budget blow-out occurred in 2008 with a $67 million increase. An additional $62 million required in 2010 pushed the original $460 million budget to $589 million. At the time of writing, the new estimated cost is $631 million, a 37% increase on the original budget, with the project now entering its fourth year of construction.[3]

The reasons given for the increased budget and extended deadline are: underestimation of security requirements for the building, asbestos issues, a failing façade, and contractor bankruptcy. When questioned about rising costs, a spokesperson for the project said that the price increase was due to the complexity of the project being larger than first anticipated, and the cost increases needed revision in respect of the project's size, complexity and length.

So, why do leaders find it necessary to resolve complex problems with a complex solution? Let's look at some possible reasons.

Justifying The Need For A Specialist

Often leaders have the mindset that if they haven't been able to solve the problem themselves, then they require the assistance of a specialist to figure out an answer.

It's not that the leader wants to blow out their budget or slow down the project's completion, but feels if they cannot solve the problem it must mean that consulting a team of specialists is the only option. Plus, working on a complex project and resolving complex problems with complex solutions makes a project appear more important, with a leader's efforts noted as being more accomplished.

Loss Of Expert Status

This thinking is a result of a leader solving complex problems in the past but now having the inability to resolve their current problems. Although this inability to resolve problems doesn't stem from the leader's lack of intellect or them not keeping up with changes; it's attributable to the increased pace of change in the world today. With change occurring this rapidly, it's near on impossible to know everything.

So, while a leader was an expert years ago and they were the 'go-to-person,' they're not now. They've lost their expert status. But the leader doesn't realise this loss. They still feel that they are knowledgeable in that specific area, so they seek to resolve the problem with complexity.

Educational Block

Leaders who are highly educated and who have years of experience also develop blind spots to simple solutions. In a philosophical sense, this aversion to simplicity is a phenomenon called Ockham's Razor (also known as Occam's Razor), which first appeared when Aristotle made himself known to the world.[4]

The basis of Ockham's Razor is that the simpler theory is more likely to be true than one that is complex. For instance, a group of web designers who have created some of the world's most interesting products and technology, such as Basecamp, Campfire and Highrise, use Ockham's Razor in daily practice.[5]

This web design group were working on a website project that had a diverse visual background, and they applied the principle of Ockham's Razor to the site navigation. This methodology resulted in what was a distracting background being toned down so that the site visitor easily gravitated towards the site message and gained a better understanding of the site quickly. This achieved the goal of further developing brand awareness of the product.

Another example of Ockham's Razor is the unique and intricate architectural design of the Guggenheim Museum in Bilbao. While this museum is breathtaking with curves and contours not seen elsewhere, it is also practical. The structure is simple to traverse, with visitors moving from A to B without difficulty, and its structural integrity has not been compromised because of its design.

Sophistication Bias

Sophistication Bias occurs when leaders cannot see the simplicity of an organisation, as they have difficulty visualising any meaningful advantage associated with this. To most leaders, an organisation needs to be sophisticated as this personifies intelligence and greatness. If, however, an organisation is simple, then it operates on 'levels of discipline,' along with 'common sense, persistence and courage' making it difficult for highly educated leaders to relate.[6]

In a complex world, educated leaders tend to look for complexity. These leaders perceive distinction and expansion as being linked to a complex structure, as to them this is competitive in an ever-changing market. However, this thinking is old and not progressive.

Today's competitive organisation needs to be simple and straightforward as this enables it to be flexible and adapt to meet changing consumer demands. As a leader, this means embracing a simple perspective as it often gives you an ability to look at problems differently; it opens your eyes to otherwise unseen possibilities.

What's the cost of complexity for a leader?

Complexity's Cost

The complex perspective can result in you missing the simple solution and either failing to solve the problem completely or wasting valuable time. The answer per se may be right in front of you, but you cannot see it as you're seeking out one that is far more comprehensive. And as you're spending all your time finding that comprehensive solution, your valuable time is being spent elsewhere, rather than on leading your team or organisation.

Consequently, the cost of complexity is significant to an organisation. When a leader's attention is not on advancing the company, then competitors can easily move in and dominate. Often these competitors are start-ups who solve problems faster and are focused on building a rapport with customers.

Start-ups typically have limited funds, so they don't have a big budget to throw at more complex solutions or the resources to spend hours looking for answers. Instead, they need to find simple solutions that are affordable. Often start-ups use their creativity because it comes free-of-charge and this creativity and ability to think outside of the traditional organisation square enables them to outwit and overtake some of the larger organisations.

So, the big slow-moving organisation with many employees and overheads, and that million-dollar budget, gets lumbered with a heavier load—a burden that erodes their profit, leaving them fighting for their market share.

Having worked with larger organisations, I've witnessed resource wastage firsthand. In these instances, rather than getting creative when a problem presents itself, leaders look to bring in a specialist or even a team of specialists to solve their problem. This strategy can cost thousands in the blink of an eye, and yet when leaders don't have these funds, they get resourceful.

A resourceful leader who looks for cost and time effective solutions to problems has a mindset that then permeates through a business. Team members also become more resourceful; whereas team members in an organisation that throws money at problems, also tend to think that they have an endless budget.

A perfect example of this occurred when a new project began in a larger organisation. The leader of the project suggested these teams differentiate themselves and their areas by decorating their space in the office. The immediate response of several of the teams was, "How much is our budget?"

There were even suggestions of needing at least a thousand each to cover expenses. And yet, resourceful teams contacted local councils and consulates and were sent a heap of colourful brochures and literature to decorate their space. The cost was nothing, and their areas looked phenomenal.

Thus, it is not so much the complexity of the project or problem but how we think and deal with these that leads to a successful outcome. It's also important to bear in mind that team members look up to their leaders, so it is instinctive for them to follow in a leader's footsteps. Thus, if a leader solves a problem by asking for a budget rather than with creativity, then it's highly likely team members will behave the same way.

However, by applying simple strategies, you can train your team or organisation to perform at a world-class level. This approach improves your business reputation, performance and margins and it gives you a competitive advantage in the marketplace as your focus is on advancement, not on putting out fires.

> Imagine a group of people struggling to push a large block of cement up a steep hill. They are sweating under the strain of exertion and the hot sun. Behind them comes a person with a wheel offering to help. The group's reply: "No thank you, we're way too busy to stop."

When we seek out a complex solution for a complex problem as a leader, we increase the heaviness of our load. We make this load a burden, one that we feel obligated to solve. When others offer help, a different perspective that is simpler than our own, we are quick to turn this down.

Often the simplest of solutions is the best. Simple solutions use less resources, they costs less and they are faster and more efficient than a complex answer.

Key Takeaways

- Einstein once said that if you can't explain something simply enough, you don't understand it. A solution to a problem does not need to be complex.

- As leaders we must be constantly asking how a problem can be broken down into simple parts to bring everyone on the journey. The simplest solution is often right in front of you and often involves picking up the phone and having a conversation.

- Complex problems don't necessarily need complex solutions; so don't overlook the simple solution.

"Genius is making complex ideas simple, not simple ideas complex."

-- Albert Einstein

CHAPTER 6

"If I Don't See My Team Working All The Time, I Question If They Are Delivering Value"

Standing on the bridge of a warship that I had been newly posted to one afternoon, I noticed that the captain seemed a little anxious. But I couldn't figure out why. The ship was sailing at a steady pace through calm waters; there were no signs of trouble—the radar, echo sounder, compass and other navigational equipment showed normal readings. Grabbing a pair of binoculars, I scanned the horizon: all clear.

The captain paced back and forth across the bridge with a perplexed look on his face. Then he mumbled something to himself before leaving the bridge. One of the crew looked over at me and said, "The captain likes it when we run around more. He prefers to see a busy bridge crew."

A few days later, the bridge crew and I worked through a number of drills during strategic manoeuvres. The captain watched on with that same perplexed look as we carried out our duties. After the drill was complete, the captain looked at me and said, "I didn't feel you showed enough, you know, urgency during that drill. You were too calm."

Today when I look back on this scenario, I realise that this captain, like so many other leaders, needed to see his team working all the time to ensure that they were delivering value. If his team were too calm and worked quietly, then to the captain it appeared as though they were not productive. Not doing 'enough.'

So, how, exactly, does this myth present itself in a business, organisation or corporate environment?

5 Past Peter

Many leaders and senior executives feel the need to micromanage their teams. This form of management involves closely observing and controlling the work that individual team members carry out.

Now while the leader sees micromanaging as the way to increase productivity, as well as know what's happening in any given project at any time, the team view this form of management as a hindrance to their creativity and a sign of distrust. Consequently, it is testing, intimidating and disheartens a team, which reduces productivity—the exact opposite of what the leader or senior executive is trying to achieve.[1]

Peter represents a perfect example of a leader who wanted to see his team working all the time. If Peter didn't see his team working, he would question if they were delivering value. Peter was the senior executive for a large corporate group based in London. He not only insisted that his team started work early, but also that they had breakfast together every morning.

Also wanting his team to be around him during the day, Peter would call them to catch up on their work progress. His most common lines when contacting a team member were, "What are you doing?" And, "Where are you?"

However, what Peter didn't realise was that every time he called, he interrupted a team member's thought process, their concentration, and their level of productivity.

The office where Peter and his team were situated overlooked the car park. So the team could see people as they arrived and left the office. Peter's micromanaging became a ritual, so the team would wait until they saw Peter walk across the car park to his vehicle before they would pack up and leave themselves. Over time, this tactic became known as leaving at "5 past Peter."

So, why do leaders need to see their team working all the time?

Well, there are several reasons and they all stem from old ways of thinking. Let's look at these now.

Ignoring Technological Advancements

With technological advancements, today's workplace is not the same as it once was. Team members don't always need to be present in the workplace to be productive—they can work from anywhere. Previously, work needed to be completed at the office as there were no systems to support remote working such as remote access, email or shared cloud storage.

Now most office workers can access company documentation, answer emails, connect with clients and create (and present!) presentations from their laptops at home or on the road. Plus, they can transfer or share files with other team members via enterprise Cloud technology, Skype and email.

So, even though an office worker is not sitting in an office in-person, they are still able to actively collaborate on projects—possibly even more effectively when you consider the time and energy saved on commuting.

However, for the leader who has moved through the ranks without such technology, it is difficult to grasp that work outside of the workplace is possible, and with relative ease. Instead, this leader needs to know what's happening, and all the time. And the only way to do this is to have their team in his line of sight.

Old Management Processes

Also, many senior executives have advanced through their career using old management principles such as Taylorism, the theory—discussed in chapter 1—which hails from the 20th Century and involves close monitoring of mass production factory workers.

Consequently, in applying this thinking to workplace practices, leaders believe that they improve the efficiency and output of a worker. Historically speaking though, this approach often resulted in workers striking and walking off the job, as many felt they were nothing but a machine put under too much scrutiny and pushed to their limitations.[2]

Applying Taylorism to thought work, where it's not as simple as monitoring people physically 'doing' tasks on a factory floor, has been met with even more resistance. This resistance, coupled with the need for a new type of workplace motivation, was the crux of Daniel Pink's 2009 book *Drive*.[3]

Research by psychologists Harry Harlow and Edward Deci in 1971 inspired Pink's theory of 'Motivation 3.0', where he posits that we need to evolve from a culture of reward and punishment (that he labels 'Motivation 2.0'). Pink speaks to the importance of autonomy, mastery and purpose being the keys to unlock motivation and world class performance in organisations.

A Culture Of Distrust

Many leaders also feel that they must see a team member working and what they are working on to believe they are doing something constructive. The nature of 'thinking' work, combined with larger workplace practices where it is difficult for a leader to monitor their staff closely, means being able to review outcomes isn't always possible.

The enormity of an organisation can then lead to a culture of distrust where a leader doesn't feel that their team is delivering value. When the team don't feel trusted, this encourages them to be less productive.

Why?

Well, distrust creates disunity between a leader and their team or an 'Us' vs 'Them' perception. When this scenario presents itself, team members may take advantage of a leader's absence to engage in activities such as chatting about their weekend and other non-work-related pursuits.

The leader of a large financial project I once worked with said that he felt his team did little when he left the office. But, when we looked at the situation more closely, it turned out that the team did quite a lot.

It's just that the leader had not articulated the value that he sought. So, without knowing what the leader wanted delivered (and by when) the team found themselves doing a lot of 'busy work' but had no way to measure the value that they were delivering.

Often when this situation occurs it is due to a lack of ability to visualise success, and many of us have difficulty creating what is sometimes referred to as 'mental models.' Even if we can create them, it can be difficult to communicate them in a way they are understood. Instead, we see what is in front of us. And even THAT varies from person to person, even when we're looking at the same thing!

For example, if a team member presents an idea to their leader without fully communicating the mental model they have in their mind, the leader may not be able to visualise the idea fully, or what their team member is truly communicating. So, they move on, leaving the idea behind.

Old-School Leadership

Then there are the leaders of organisations that are stuck in the past. These groups may still have dress-codes, a 'do what you are told' approach and cultures of hoarding information.

This type of behaviour is quite prevalent in business today, and it occurs because many leaders are Baby Boomers (born between 1945-1964) or Gen-Xers (born between 1965-1980). These leaders, as a result of their own experience, may have completely different work values, attitudes and expectations than younger generations.[4]

For example, a previous colleague of mine, a young man in his mid-twenties, started work in a data centre as a technology consultant managing the computer back-end for the company. The facility resembled a bunker: thick walls, no windows, and series of security doors protected its contents. No customers ventured into this area as it contained highly confidential data storage.

When this young man first started working in the data centre, he wore a suit and tie to work every day. Then, after a few weeks, he decided that he would relax a little and go to work without his tie, because, once inside the work building, no-one but his colleagues saw him.

Entering the building tieless was not an issue. But, when the young man's boss saw him without a tie, the first thing he asked was, "Where is your tie?" When the young man responded, "Oh, I just decided, you know, not to wear one today. I find I can think better without it, and figured as we were not facing into customers it would be okay." His boss glared at him and said, "You should always wear your tie."

Given these scenarios, what's the cost of questioning the value that your team are delivering?

Presenteeism

Ignoring technological advancements, following old management processes that facilitate a culture of distrust and implementing old-school leadership tactics lead to an escalation of 'presenteeism'—where team members are at work, but they're not productive.

Presenteeism is estimated to cost the Australian economy over $34 billion every year, with increased workloads and demands, and job insecurity pushing many organisation employees to their limits. Therefore, rather than being absent, many employees turn up for work but do less, due to feeling physically or mentally exhausted, or that their leader lacks faith in their ability to perform.[5]

Another issue is that the workplace has changed dramatically over the years. In the 'industrial economy' workers made products and in the 'service economy' these workers provided services. But today's economy is knowledge-based, making it harder to place value on, and to navigate, day to day work.

Knowledge workers receive payment for what they know, rather than for what they do. Therefore, the challenge for them is how to demonstrate tangible evidence of completed work—apart from answering emails and attending meetings. So, when this job role is misunderstood, attention focuses on answering trivial emails, and knowledge workers do not apply themselves to more meaningful and profound tasks that fulfil their own intellectual needs or their employer's expectations.

For instance, in a study of U.S business, it was discovered that on average more than 300 emails are received weekly by a business employee and that employees typically check their email 36 times daily. Plus, it then takes the employee approximately 16-minutes to refocus on their work after answering emails.[6]

Also, the average employee attends around 60 meetings monthly with half of the meetings considered as wasted time. These meetings equate to more than 30 hours of unproductive time throughout a month, with these lost hours estimated to cost U.S business more than $37 billion annually.

So, as you can see, overcoming presenteeism isn't an easy task and forces us to rethink how we define a productive day (does 'inbox zero' sound familiar?). Many companies have tried different approaches, but most have found challenges. Let's look at some case studies.

The 20% Rule

Several larger companies such as Latvia and Google have brought in the 20% rule, where 20% of an employee's working time is used to work on whatever that employee wants to, providing the employee shares this work with their colleagues and leader. However, in saying this, the companies are very flexible as to what constitutes work because they've found that some of the best ideas come from completely random searches.

This flexible approach has had surprising (and valuable) outcomes in organisations who have employed this practice. As well as creating innovative products, many employees chose to work on issues that annoyed them—for example, company processes that took too long to deliver results.[7]

Innovation can and does contribute to an organisation's success, and yet when given the flexibility to work on what they want, employees take up time solving problems that would otherwise go unsolved, which can perpetuate a busy work cycle that still ultimately leads to no time for innovation.

The important thing about 20% time is that employees are given the time and space to focus on it without undue influence from management eager to see people working hard.

Flexible Workplace Practice

Yahoo also used a flexible work practice where their employees could work from home. However, the new CEO Marissa Mayer removed the policy and insisted that over 12,000 work-from-home employees came into the office. This move in 2013 sparked debate, but Yahoo reported that the move increased employee engagement, with teams thriving.

Yet, two years on, it appears that Yahoo employees have drifted back, on occasions, to working from home. Companies that have embraced work-from-home practices are said to be able to encourage top talent to work for them, and that workplace productivity improves significantly with the promise of a work/life balance.

Now, while studies show that the complete work-from-home policy is slim (about 2.4% of the workforce), the number of employees that work-from-home 'on occasions' has risen to over 60%.[8]

Accommodating Travel Policy

Another company I mentored, who had employees flying all over the world to work with clients, used to have a travel policy in place where the employee took time out from the office to recuperate from their flight. For example, if you worked for this company and you flew to the United States on their behalf, when you returned to Australia you would be able to take the time off you needed to recover from travelling.

If you flew in on a Sunday night for instance, then you could opt to come into work on Tuesday. And the company did not specify how long you could take off; they just trusted your judgement.

When I investigated further, I found that some employees were taking a lot of time off. They would fly back from Denver, say, on Sunday afternoon and wouldn't come into the office until Thursday.

When challenged, the employees (many of whom were management-level) presented actual calculations to justify this time off. This challenge prompted the company to change their policy. Instead of giving their employees time off to recuperate from travel, they now expected all employees to be at work the day after their flight. And this case is by no means isolated.

In cases like these, one of the biggest concerns for the organisations was whether they were being taken advantage of, or whether employees were genuinely using time away from the office well, whether that be recovering from travel or doing meaningful work that benefited from being undisturbed by an office environment. In the case of doing meaningful work, the type of work carried out by employees is key. Is it deep or busy work?

Deep Work Vs. Busy Work

Deep work happens when you can focus your attention on a task that is mentally demanding. If you harness the ability to do this, then you'll not only achieve outstanding results, but you'll also harness a skill that is becoming rare in a world full of distractions.

Busy work, on the other hand, is what many of us do daily. We run around checking emails, going to meetings, reading articles that teach us how to do tasks, upgrading software, and cleaning up our workspace. So, while we're busy, we're not being truly productive.

Team members can rush around all day every day doing busy work, often so they can be 'seen' working. But are they using their mental capabilities or are they just the robotic factory worker?

Picture a factory setting with a conveyer belt moving items along it at pace. A small issue happens at the start of the belt causing a domino effect of problems all the way down the line. To the extent that items are falling off and piling up haphazardly. Workers are scratching their heads looking confused, not sure how to resolve what is becoming an increasingly disastrous situation.

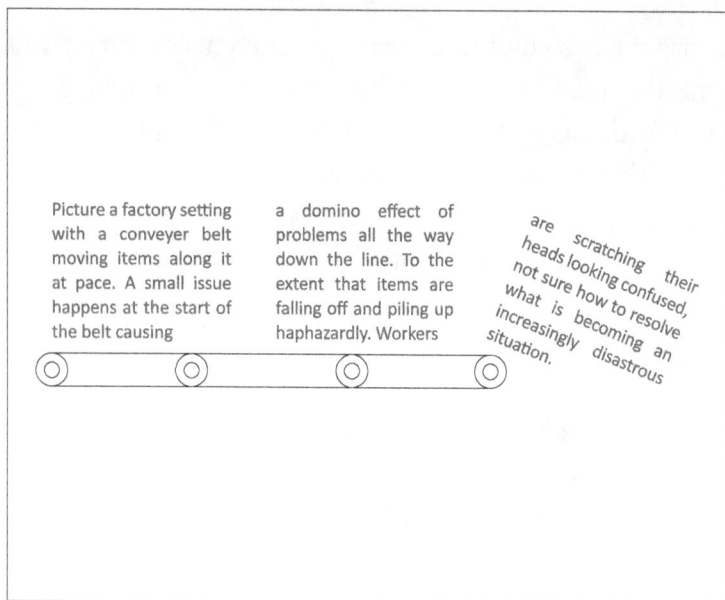

They are busy, but they're not delivering value because they are just going through the motions. This lack of perception, and inability to recognise problems and to then troubleshoot them, is 'busy work.' However, if the workers in the factory took the time to solve the issue of why products were falling off the conveyor (possibly even pausing the conveyer), then they would be carrying out 'deep work.' This deep work may not look like work at all, it may well happen out of hours or on the phone, invisible to the immediate eye but delivering immense value.

In a business sense, most team members and employees are running around doing busy work. So, they are not creative, and they're not resolving problems. As a result, it's a little like the factory workers with the products falling off all around them—no productivity occurs in the workplace, and ignoring little problems in favour of 'looking busy' can result in far bigger problems that result in losing market share or going under completely.

Key Takeaways

- 'Busy work' is not valuable work.

- Teams build great cultures by taking the time to get to know each other. By facilitating a workplace culture that embraces flexibility within reason and seeks to develop a deep work ethic, we can encourage leaders to move away from the old way of thinking.

  "When you know your biorhythms, you work well. Just remember that everyone is different, so this makes the construct of the 9-5 office an impediment on productivity."

  -- Daniel Pink

CHAPTER 7

"I Need To Have A Single Point Of Contact Who Has The Ability To Resolve Any Issue Within Their Span Of Control"

Early in 1983, the Challenger space shuttle prepared for its main voyage. The shuttle—developed after five successful Columbia space shuttle voyages—had a lighter frame and blankets instead of tiles to protect areas of the vehicle. Plus, engineers increased maximum thrust performance and used a lightweight external fuel tank.

These tweaks reduced the weight of the shuttle and gave it more power. These improvements allowed the ship and four crew members to deploy a series of data and tracking satellites, creating better space shuttle communication for future missions before they safely returned to Earth.[1]

Three years later, the Challenger, which had successfully carried out nine voyages since its maiden voyage, took off on its next expedition. This mission was special because for the first time a civilian was aboard the spacecraft. However, the crew and the craft never made it into space.

Just 73 seconds after taking off, the vessel experienced a mid-air disaster that resulted in an explosion. The hundreds of people who stood watching the lift-off, some who were family and friends of the crew on board the shuttle, were left speechless as they witnessed the craft catch fire, leave a plume of smoke in the air, and then fragment before plummeting into the ocean.

Millions of people watched the Challenger's live telecast around the world. The crew—six astronauts and the school teacher who had earned her spot on the shuttle via the NASA Teacher in Space Program—all lost their lives.[2]

After the incident, U.S. President Ronald Reagan launched a commission into why this tragic event occurred. The findings astounded many—an O-ring on the right-hand rocket booster failed in the extremely cold weather. This failure resulted in hot gas escaping and damaging the orbiter's external fuel tank and the gear linked to the tank booster. Yet this problem had been reported by a contractor when shuttle testing.[3]

So, what went wrong?

PowerPoint Problems

Shuttle-testing reports presented in PowerPoint trivialised important information and made it difficult to understand complex engineering data. NASA management also relied on these PowerPoint reports. Thus, a single point of contact existed between management and the engineers, which set the mission up for failure.[4]

In a study of NASA PowerPoints, researchers estimate that this style of presentation has been responsible for two space incidents—the 1983 Challenger shuttle explosion and the 2003 Columbia shuttle disaster—killing all astronauts on board both shuttles. Both the bulleted nature of the PowerPoint and the over exuberance of NASA management contributed to these disasters, as it's easy to overlook problems when buried in other trivial information. Experts also suggest that engineering reports are too difficult to present in PowerPoint, if not impossible.

Reflecting on these incidents in a business sense highlights that it can be risky or even dangerous to rely on a single point of contact when working on complex projects.

But how does this situation occur in an organisation, you ask?

Well, it presents itself in several ways, and the most prominent stem from a project leader who believes they need to know every minute detail in order to report progress to stakeholders.

Understanding Project Complexity

A security program project I recently led represents a perfect example of this belief.

I was in a meeting with stakeholders. We were discussing the progress of the project when one executive asked a question that stumped me.

"What's the difference between the two types of encryption standards?" he asked.

I was unprepared for the question, which left me red-faced and feeling inadequate and I was also disappointed in myself for not knowing the answer. At the time, I remember thinking that I should have known all the answers because, after all, I was leading the project.

Of course, later I realised that it was impossible for me to have all the answers. Firstly, the project was far too big and extremely complex—I would have needed to be a software specialist and understand several computer languages to have the answers to complex questions like these at hand. Secondly, the time that it would have taken to come up to speed on knowledge like encryption standards would have taken days, if not months, for me to fully understand so I could convey the information professionally.

What I should have done when asked about the difference between encryption standards was refer the questioner to the person in my team who had that knowledge on hand. But I didn't, and this was a well-learned lesson on my part.

So, am I the only leader who has been in this situation?

Absolutely not! Many leaders have experienced the same as I did. Some may well have had the information on hand due to spending time researching the complex details—time that could have been spent leading rather than knowing.

The 'All Knowing' Leadership Mindset

As leaders, we sometimes feel obligated to know everything. Therefore, we aim to be that single point of contact when leading complex change. And yet, when we critically look at this situation, it quickly becomes evident that being the single point of contact is a recipe for disaster.

I have seen leaders frantically trying to cram information into their brains before flying off to meet customers, and they often expect their teams to bring them up to speed on all areas of the project. They will also demand that a PowerPoint is prepared for them so that they can present summarised facts and figures.

But, as witnessed with the space shuttle disasters, these PowerPoints do not adequately convey the right information. Plus, trying to understand too much as a leader can lead to executive overload, where you feel overwhelmed by the amount of information that you need to absorb, pushing your stress levels to the extreme. Not to mention the stress levels of the experts in the field who take time out of their deadline-driven work to share their knowledge and create the PowerPoint packs.

Another problem that occurs for the leader striving to be the single point of contact is this leader is not the expert but simply a conduit through which the information flows. So, rather than sharing from their own perspective, the leader is merely sharing memorised notes, as they have not lived the experience themselves.

Consequently, this methodology opens the leader up to misinterpretation of the facts—a little like the popular children's game where a message is whispered to each player down a line, with the final message heard by the group being quite different from the original one.

Misinterpreting Information

Many years ago, a leader I coached misinterpreted information with regularity. It wasn't that this person had difficulty retaining information, but rather they could not communicate what they had learned effectively to others.

So, they would go to a workshop where new information was conveyed and then come out of that session keen to share their learning experience. But the information they shared was often not even close to the original because they had put their own spin on what they had learned—they had interpreted this information very differently.

It's a given that we will all delete, distort and generalise information; we do it all the time. It is a factor of human behaviour that relates directly to our own lived experiences, cultural background and personalities. We cannot help but view the world from our own unique perspective.

Thus, if we rely on one person to convey important facts about something complex, then it's highly likely the information subsequently communicated will be flawed. This scenario occurs because this one person has a set of beliefs, values, experiences and memories and they apply these unconsciously when presenting information or attempting to solve a problem. Which, when you think about a complex project with complicated issues, can be dangerous?

Why does this myth surface in an organisation?

Leaders As Experts

If you take a step back and look at the structure of businesses before computers and the Internet became popular, you'll discover that back then a leader knew a lot. This leader was the 'go-to person'—they had more knowledge and were a powerful force because they were a specialist. So, in the past, it was possible for one person to solve even the most intricate of problems in an organisation.

But today's organisation is more elaborate. There are more departments and more people with specialist knowledge because business has developed along with technology, and organisations are far more complex than they once were. As a result, a single leader cannot possibly know everything. Instead, they must rely on a team.

But, for a leader who has been in an executive role throughout this change, it's difficult to modify how they've successfully operated for years. For them to adopt new habits means unlearning their beliefs, experiences and, in some cases, values, while adopting new ones that are effective in the business that has evolved, and is continuing to evolve.

Many leaders are great at learning, but they have never learned how to unlearn, which stops them from effectively using new information.

Leader Power Sources

Another problem that surfaces for leaders is that they are often used to being the person their team turns to when a crisis occurs. So, when they are no longer the 'go-to' person for everything work-related, it can make them feel redundant and no longer needed in the workplace, which can erode confidence.

However, expertise is only one source of power available to a leader, and the leader of the future needs to draw upon multiple sources of power and influence. In any given day, leaders are called upon to tap into their power as an expert, but they also have more power in other areas than they realise. A big source of power is personal power—who you are as a person and how you relate to others.

By using your personal power as a leader, you effectively guide your organisation to successful outcomes, simply by who you are rather than solely on what you know. Plus, if you've been in an executive role for many years, then those relationships that you have developed through personal power will far outweigh any expert knowledge that quickly becomes out-dated.

Economist John Galbraith defines power as having three sources of power—personality, property and organisation.

'Personality' refers directly to leadership where persuasive ability leads others. Those who can speak publicly and have an enigmatic image typically captivate the attention of others far more readily than someone who cannot convey their ideas well and has poor presentation.[5]

The second source of power for a leader, 'property,' is the organisation, department or project that they preside over. By owning this organisation, department or project, the leader has wealth and success.

The third source of power, 'organisation,' is the source that is the most important in today's busy world.

Why?

Well, this source of power enables the other sources of power to exist. Without organisation, personality and property are merely conceptual. Organisation brings everything together, creating a system of parts that work in tandem. Effective organisation takes away the risk of a single point of contact.

So, what cost do executives who use a single point of contact typically experience?

Single Point Cost

Executives that employ the old-fashioned single point of contact methodology in their organisation encounter an array of issues such as missing valuable information, accidents occurring as well as disasters—as NASA discovered with their space shuttles.

Albert Einstein once said that if he were given an hour to save Earth, then he'd spend 59 minutes defining the problem and only a minute resolving it. I would expand on that and suggest spending the first 10 minutes identifying the key people to contribute to the resolution.

Unfortunately, most organisations don't heed these wise words. Instead, they are too eager to get results, so they often overlook the root cause of the problem. Plus, many don't ask for the input of others, they fly solo.

This scenario occurs in the development of new products or processes. A solo effort that does not take in contributions from others results in wasted resources, missed opportunities, and following initiatives that are not strategically aligned.[6]

Plus, the single point of contact philosophy can also take a leader down the wrong path so that they employ a siloed mentality, where departments or individuals within these departments refuse to share information. This mindset reduces morale, company productivity and the overall operation of the organisation.[7]

I have witnessed this scenario countless times.

One example that resonates is a rapid planning workshop that I ran several years ago where a single point of contact caused issues. At the time, we were aiming to create a timeline for the design, development and launch of a product into the marketplace.

The whole room consisted of several representatives from each department, and all were collaborating on ideas, possibilities and preferred outcomes. That is, all except for one department. Only one senior executive turned up to represent their specialist area, which had a significant role to play in achieving the project outcome.

Now, while this senior executive was insightful, they also had generalised knowledge—the type that comes from gathering information from their experts on the fly, not from their own specialist knowledge or experience. As a result, this executive could not contribute to the detailed discussion that was needed to properly plan this initiative.

As a result, my alarm bells sounded.

Foreseeing problems arising from this limited view of the project in a key area, all at the meeting decided to reconvene later to have more representatives for this area to be present. We also worked to create a visual representation of the work in a common area of the building, allowing others to see and contribute.

This strategy enabled us to clarify key components of the project, reduce risk and ensure we could make informed decisions based on a number of perspectives, not just one. What we also achieved was buy-in from that area with the contributors acting as empowered champions for the change.

When many people contribute their ideas and thoughts, and they discuss options, then the best outcomes are found in the shortest time. This strategy leads to greater business productivity, effective time management and constructive use of resources.

However, when using a single of point of contact, then this leads to the finger of blame coming into play if the outcome is not favourable.

Pointing The Finger Of Blame

We all know the finger of blame, some of us better than others.

This finger typically gets pointed when making an error. So, as an executive, when you are the single point of contact, then ultimately you also take full responsibility for any outcomes that result from any action on your part.

Whereas when you are the leader of a team who presents the facts and findings for others to discuss, the finger of blame can no longer be pointed at one person. Instead, the group which made the decisions carries the burden of any errors—this shared accountability results in an empowered team and at the same time lightens the personal and professional load for an executive or leader.

> Many
> know this scene well. A serious
> group of executives sitting around a board-
> room table. Something has happened. Paper-
> work is piled up as the group work through what
> seems like a mountain of correspondence. They
> are angry. And also puzzled. All they want to
> know is: "Who is responsible?" The
> answer: Everyone.

Reflecting on my naval days, I can recall when a significant event occurred back in the '90s. A ship caught fire, which resulted in the injury and death of several crew members. Of course, the media was quick to put the incident into the spotlight, and they wanted to know who was responsible; they needed to point that finger of blame at someone.

And yet, rather than name an individual, the Chief of the Navy simply said in a press conference that the problem was systemic, which resulted from practices that review. This answer made me proud as an officer because it upheld my values and beliefs that problems are created and solved by 'many' rather than 'one.'

The same scenario is also true for the *Titanic* disaster. Sure, an iceberg was the ship's final undoing. But, if we look at the other facts, then we also find that the ship was travelling too fast, in poor visibility—a recipe for disaster.[8]

Navigating a ship through challenging waters is a little like driving a car in foggy conditions—you typically slow down to safely drive on. The *Titanic* was said to have a top speed of 23 knots. According to data at the time of the collision, the ship travelled at 22.3 knots. And yet, the ship's crew had received several warnings about icebergs in the area.

Other contributing factors to the disaster included poor design, so when the ship took on water, it spread too fast. Also, there were not enough lifeboats to accommodate the number of guests on board, and the crew who operated the life vessels were not well-versed in the use of the safety equipment. Consequently, too few people made it to the lifeboats, and some boats launched with nobody on board.

There are also suggestions that an early fire in the engine room of the ship had not been put out. This fire subsequently caused significant damage.

So, if we look at the *Titanic* disaster in a business sense, we can see that there are several events that all contributed to the disaster, not just one. Also, the captain appears to have been the single point of contact, taking on all the responsibility instead of collaborating with others to deal with (or prevent) the series of events that led to the disaster.

Key Takeaway

- Our rapidly changing world presents more and more complex problems. Solving these is only achieved through collaboration and information sharing, also known as radical transparency. This transparency reduces risk as more than one person injects their way of thinking into a project, which results in team discussion and shared accountability.

"Visual management moves the invisible to the visible with superheroes now needing to work together in teams, rather than as individuals."

-- Emma Sharrock

CHAPTER 8

"I'm Able To Convey My Vision And Plan Clearly, But Often My Team Just Doesn't Get It"

T he team and executives arrived at the meeting room bright and early in the morning. All were very enthusiastic about the day ahead.

This strategy session was going to be different from the many they had attended previously; it was going to be far more meaningful as collectively they would be sharing their concepts and progress, with a view to generating new ideas and fresh enthusiasm across the organisation.

But what transpired was not the same for everyone in the room.

Wanting to know how everyone felt about the workshop, I took time out to chat to a handful of attendees, both executives and team members. Their reactions were mixed.

The executives thought the day was a resounding success. One executive effervesced at the strategy session's accomplishments. "It was brilliant," he said. "We communicated our vision with precision, and everyone in the room was on the same page. You must watch the video. It's brilliant."

He thrust a CD into my hand, and I smiled and thanked him for the opportunity.

The team members, on the other hand, were left feeling bewildered and even more confused after the event than they had been before it started. "We just don't get it," they said. "The whole session made no sense, and we were exhausted by the end of it."

I was astounded. How could all these people be in the same room and yet have such different recollections of the day?

Wanting to get to the bottom of this, I took the CD and found a quiet area to sit and watch it. Loading the CD and pressing play, I felt excited; after all, the executive who had given me the video had claimed it was inspiring.

The first image that popped onto my screen was of a pie chart. In this chart were a whole bunch of numbers that related to profit and growth. None of it made any sense.

Then the video panned to one of the executives, who stood up and made their way to the front of the group. This executive proceeded to explain what they had achieved. Then, one-by-one, the other executives got up and proceeded to do the same as the first.

By the end of the video, I fully understood why the teams weren't inspired as I honestly had no idea what the vision or plan was for the strategy session, either.

So, why had this strategy session turned out so differently for the executives and the teams?

Well, firstly the executives had worked on their strategy together—they'd fully internalised the meaning of the vision, and they'd shared concepts, so they knew what each meant and how these interconnected. The team, however, had been left out of the picture. All ideas presented at the strategy session were new to them—they were not involved in the creation of these.

Secondly, it was not so much the information presented, but the way the executives presented the information. The information was from an executive's perspective, as in "I've done this, and I've done that." So, it wasn't inclusive, as it didn't consider the audience.

I guess it's like me talking to a group using nothing but technical jargon and acronyms, and then expecting the group to understand every word. Most people would need clarification.

In a business sense, this incident exposes the myth that an executive or team leader feels that they've conveyed their vision clearly, but their team just doesn't get it.

So how does this truth present in the workplace?

Isn't It Obvious?

What happens, in most cases, is the executives do have a clear vision—it's just that they fail to adequately explain this in a way that their teams understand.

I often find that executives and team leaders use a common saying when working on projects they understand but have difficulty explaining, this being "isn't it obvious."

If this saying comes out, then I know that what they are referring to isn't obvious at all. Instead, they need to explain themselves better.

An easy way to understand how this happens is to think of a song. Pick a song, any song, and play that song to yourself in your head.

Then find someone who is close by, and tap that song out on a desktop, bench or any hard, flat surface. Next, see if the person who is listening can guess the song. I bet that they can't.

Nursery rhymes and even common songs such as 'Happy Birthday' are difficult to understand when tapped out. This situation occurs because you have all the information in your head that you need to understand the song. But the person who is listening has only a fragment of that information, and they are relying on you to explain it to them, which you cannot do clearly.

The same also happens when a leader tries to explain their vision and plan to their team. The team leader has all the information—it's in their head, so they live it, feel it and even breathe it. But the team members only receive a fragment of the information from their leader.

As a result, a leader encounters four distinct issues when defining their vision and plan:

1) Their team has a lack of alignment due to them not understanding the business direction,

2) The team is confused when it comes down to priorities,

3) The leader has a clear strategy, but poor execution

4) The strategy is understood, but day-to-day priorities prevent execution from happening effectively, or at all.

Let's look at each of these issues in greater detail.

Lack of Alignment

Leaders typically adopt the 'I've told you once' view when it comes to explaining their plan and vision. They have this expectation of their staff that they'll automatically know what to do.

But, in most cases, the team has little or no idea whatsoever because the businesses priorities are not clear to them, and this results in a lack of alignment between the leader, teams and the organisation.

When a lack of alignment exists in a company or department, then it creates a rift. So, instead of the teams happily working towards common goals, they head off on different tangents without a shared sense of purpose.

Thus, time, energy and talents get wasted, deadlines get missed, and the company's performance declines.[1]

Team Confusion

Confusion results from a lack of clarification when it comes to ideas. See, we as humans think much faster than we speak or write. So, when we get an idea, this then turns into many other thoughts, and concepts then develop.

But we cannot process these thoughts quickly enough. So, when we write these down, we only capture a small percentage of our original idea.

Consequently, many leaders know what they want to say. But when it comes to sharing their thoughts, they lose much of their original concept due to new thoughts emerging.

Clear Strategy, Poor Execution

If you have a great strategy, but as a leader you have no plan in place for the execution of this strategy, then at some stage during the project, it's going to cause issues. It's easy for leaders to assume that their team know what they are doing, especially if the team don't voice their opinions and concerns.

Most team members will do their job because, for many, this is what they've done for years. The team and you as a leader assume roles, and these centre on what you've previously done. Efforts get duplicated without the team or the leader realising.

For instance, let's say you're managing the roll-out of new business branding. You've decided on your business colours, designed your new logo and stationery, as well as hired a public relations team for the big unveil.

But you haven't put any thought into how execution will happen. So, while the teams have been working towards creating the new branding, their efforts are uncoordinated, with vital tasks missed. Therefore, with the launch fast approaching, there is a good chance you will not be ready.

Business Running Overrules Change

Often a business leader will buy into the idea of executing strategic change but will still tend to focus a large part of their attention on running the business. Implementing change uses resources, and those resources are scarce and often used to solve the immediate performance targets and issues, with the long-term future being ignored in the process.

However, many businesses are finding it difficult to keep up with change. So, they are now turning their attention to automating processes and freeing up time to focus more on strategic change.

But if they are going to adopt this approach, then they need to keep their teams in the loop. Planning and implementing changes without informing and involving those involved can create significant issues.

Toast-Making Mayhem

Recently I ran a workshop where I asked the attendees to describe how they make toast. Each person had just three minutes to draw their total toast-making steps on post-it notes.

By the end of the three minutes, the results were astoundingly diverse. One participant made toast in just four steps, the majority took seven, while another person took 15 steps.

This activity opened our eyes to how each of us thinks differently to the other. If we had such a variety of processes for making something as simple as toast, then what chance do we have of successfully navigating a complex change in the workplace?

Albert Einstein once said, "If you cannot explain it simply, then you don't know it well enough."

Communication is the key to the successful operation of any organisation, and that can be as simple as talking to colleagues about their weekend to discussing complex processes or troubleshooting and resolving problems. But I've seen many leaders stumble when trying to convey their message and these are very switched-on people.

One incident I recall happened on-site at a meeting. We had run through most of the materials for the session, and everyone in the room had an opportunity to share their updates.

The department executive had arrived late and was standing, so I asked if he'd like to add anything. He replied, "No not really." Then he talked for the next 15 minutes about nothing that related to the meeting. This situation was a little awkward and left many people in the room confused.

Had this department executive, like so many other leaders, thought clearly about what he wanted to say before the meeting, then his message could have been delivered with far greater clarity. It could have even been a profound moment.

So, why did this incident occur?

Information Overload

We are constantly bombarded with information. When you get up in the morning, you either turn on the radio, the TV or your computer, or you read the newspaper while drinking your coffee and eating your breakfast.

You might turn on the radio while in your car driving to work or listen to the radio while on the tram or you'll look at your mobile—every time you turn on one of these devices or read the news, information bombards you.

Then when you get to work, this information overload continues. You need to read emails and respond to these, carry out research, read reports and memos, and then attend meetings.

For a team member, the company vision and strategy are only a small portion of the information they consume. Consequently, they may not retain the details of the strategy well, which means when it comes time to convey it to others, as Albert Einstein said, "they don't know it well enough."

Landing The Message

It doesn't matter whether you're sending out a message to your consumer as a business or out to your team, you need to repeat this message so that it resonates. Research indicates that slogans work because people remember these along with advertising jingles when searching for a product or service.[2]

For a message to land and be absorbed, the consumer needs to be exposed to it (see, hear, feel) at least *seven* times—although recent research indicates it may even be more than this.

The workplace is no different. On average, your team or you as a leader will need to see information at least five times before you absorb it and are able to use it.

This is a challenge for many leaders as repetition of messages may seem wasteful and inefficient, but in fact it is one of the most valuable activities you can do as a leader.

Communicator And Receiver Issues

If we look critically at how we communicate and receive information, then we can understand how this simple process can sometimes cause problems, especially in a busy workplace.

Let's say John and Mary are discussing the latest vision and plan. Mary, the leader, tells John where she sees the business heading in the future and how she'd like John to be a part of that change.

But John hears only a portion of Mary's message because he's thinking about the project he's currently working on and that beeping noise in the background. Plus, Mary isn't talking loud enough, so John has missed parts of what she said, and now John doesn't want to appear rude by asking her to repeat herself.

Also, John may not respond well to auditory learning—he may be a visual, kinesthetic or auditory digital learner. So, to effectively impart her message to John, Mary needs to take into consideration how she is communicating her message to him.

I often find in workshops that getting people to draw simple images like a baby defines how we all think differently. Even though we all know what a baby looks like, every baby drawn is completely different. Some have no hair, others have spikes or even curls. Some babies might have one tooth and a smile, and others have no teeth and are crying.

This perception of a baby comes from our experiences and also how we use our brain.

Delayed Information Recall

Years ago, I attended a productivity course that focused on memory and why we forget important information but retain trivia, like those '80s pop songs and who sang them. It comes down to having trust in your ability to remember and not putting yourself on the spot to deliver information.

If you're stressed or frustrated, which often results when you 'need to know important information now,' then you cannot recall the information you need. You panic, and you consequently don't trust yourself to remember relevant information.

If you're relaxed and chatting about trivial information with friends, random lyrics and facts seem to pop easily into your head. It's because you are calm and not under any pressure to retrieve that information.

I recently experienced the former situation while running a training session. I was in search of a common technical term, but it wasn't a complex one at all. But it was important to mention to ensure we were all on the same page about a particular concept. Frustrated, I paused and said, "Oh, I cannot find the right word… It's when you put a system in place that tracks what's going on in a system."

One attendee smiled at me and then said, "Oh, you mean system monitoring." Smiling back at them, I replied 'That's it!' I'm sure they thought I was testing them.

So, what is the cost to the business when you as a leader don't convey a clear vision and strategy?

Poor Communication

Not being able to share your vision and plan with others confuses your team.

Poor communication is a huge cost, and it shows up in several ways. Maybe the business has a lack of priorities, with staff wasting time and effort doing work that won't lead to results. Also, as a result of spending time on low value work staff ends up having low work morale and missing important objectives.

Overall, it can mean that key messages crucial to high performance get missed due to this confusion. Meanwhile, you as a leader feel confident that you've effectively communicated your vision and plan to your team, but the message isn't landing.

In this confusion, organisational goals get missed completely, and this, in turn, can result in lost revenue, poor productivity and erosion of the bottom line. Plus, no-one in the workplace knows what they are doing and why they are doing it.

As a facilitator, I've witnessed this cost first-hand. But many leaders find it difficult to relate to because they genuinely feel that the issue lies with their team and not them.

For example, during a team workshop, I had a leader approach me. She was concerned about her team and their lack of morale. At the time she said, "I get a little bit tired of people on my team asking about the 'why.' Shouldn't they just be getting on with it?"

My response was, "If your team know the 'why' behind their work, then they are more likely to 'get on with it', reach targets and perform at a higher level."

Creating cohesion and common goals allows your team and you as a leader to make micro decisions throughout a project. By knowing the 'why' behind a project, this leads to you changing or making different choices because you understand the overall goal. Without knowing the 'why,' the decisions made may not benefit the project.

For example, let's say you're building a car. If you know 'why' you are building the car, then you'll build it a certain way. You wouldn't put family vehicle components in a race car or vice versa.

But without knowing the 'why,' then the parts for the vehicle may not adequately meet the needs of the consumer buying the vehicle, or these parts may make the vehicle unaffordable. As a result, the project fails to meet consumer needs, and this could be detrimental to the business with poor sales and overspending on the build.

Understanding the 'why' puts everyone working on a project on the same page. They develop a bond—a cohesion—that enables them to achieve greater results.

If I asked you
to picture a shape in your
head right now, what is the first thing
that comes to mind? A circle? A triangle? A
hexagon? Imagine if this shape in my head was my vision and we
were in a room with 20 others. There is potential for 22
different shapes to be imagined. When you describe
success in vague terms, it's like saying you are thinking
of a shape, giving no more information than that.
While a room full of different shapes and
patterns might mean diversity. It also means
inconsistent execution of the vision.

Left Versus Right

When you communicate the 'why' to your team, this can be broken down into individual parts, and this then coveys a clearer vision and plan.

This process makes it easier for everyone to grasp and understand because you've simplified the message. Instead of it being a lot of information to absorb, it's now in sections, which makes it easier to process and to retain.

This form of message delivery is important because, as we've already discovered, we all think very differently to each other—some of us use more of the left side of the brain (logic, data facts), while others use more of the right side of the brain (creativity). Plus, it also depends on your area of expertise and life experience.

As a leader, you can come up with a vision and a plan, but you need your team to experience the same vision so they can feel a part of the plan. This involvement allows your team to avoid any confusion.

Being on the same page is vital in any organisation no matter its size.

As a leader, we often think that everyone shares the same vision as we do. And yet, if we could see the thoughts of others, we'd discover that they have very different views to ours. Failure to clarify a business vision can result in confusion and lost opportunities.

Adequately clarifying a business vision and plan can see you as a leader soar to greater heights—your team works better together, they are more productive and utilise their time more efficiently, and the results delivered are exceptional. Plus, it is rewarding to achieve goals that may otherwise seem elusive and fulfilling to reach these goals together as on organisation.

Reflecting on my time at sea with the navy, one of the most effective times a ship's crew pull together is when in combat. During this time the captain uses a simple, but effective, priority system called 'fight, move, float.'

If the priority is to fight, then the crew's focus is manning weapons systems. If the priority changes to move, then the focus becomes the engine room and navigational posts. If the priority is to float, the crew focus on firefighting and damage control activities such as plugging up holes.

Everyone knows their role in every priority situation, and there is no room for misalignment or confusion.

When in combat, the crew share the same vision—to protect, defend and survive. All of the crew work together to achieve this 'why' because they live and experience it daily—it's their sense of purpose and duty as a sailor.

Key Takeaway

- It's important that, as a leader, you concentrate on spending time communicating your vision, so everyone in your organisation joins you on that journey. By involving all team members, you create a mindset shift of involvement, unification and striving to reach common goals that work towards your objective. This communication is more critical than 'running the business,' as without it you may find that there is no business.

"Planning is like worrying, never do it alone."

-- Emma Sharrock

CHAPTER 9

"My Team's Performance Is Fine; It's The Other Teams Who Need Performance Help"

My coaching takes me to some beautiful locations—sprawling parklands, breathtaking cityscapes, and magnificent historic buildings. But none is as special as coaching on an island with enticing ocean vistas that stretch for miles. This location is remarkable and makes for the perfect backdrop to evoke harmonious change.

Recalling this stunning location brings back memories of the teams that I worked with at that time. Coaching two teams from the same organisation at varying levels of performance compounded the team segregation that existed within the business.

Team one and their leader were at the top of their echelon —they were high performers—and as such, they felt that they knew all there was to know. This team didn't recognise the need to change or adapt to a fast-moving world. Instead, this team and its leader felt that it was the other teams who were letting them down. These other teams were the ones who needed to adapt.

Unfortunately, this attitude had resulted in this team's performance slipping, and this was having an impact on the business.

The second team, however, had a far lower performance rating. Thus, this team were eager to achieve better results, and they were hungry to learn.

So, while the location was calm and soothing, it was far from serene. The beautiful scenery concealed a battle that was brewing between teams.

During coaching, the high-performing team and their leader carried out self-assessments that I facilitated. The team rated themselves exceptionally high in several areas, even where their work was falling behind. This team were not meeting targets, which had a profound effect on other departments which relied on them to pull through.

When I asked for evidence to support this team's claims (which is a standard part of the self-assessment process), they could not produce it. Some team members even challenged me by questioning why I was criticising their behaviour.

This defensive line immediately set off my alarm bells and got me thinking about the Dunning Kruger effect—a cognitive bias where people who aren't performing at their best fail to recognise their inadequacies.[1]

Research suggests that only 39% of employees handle constructive criticism well, and this is often where they want to learn about their shortfalls so that they can correct and improve them. However, in this case, the high-performing team and their leader refused to acknowledge that their skills needed any improvement.

When these situations occur—where leaders and teams refuse to look at themselves critically—then it's my job to enlighten them. But sometimes this is far easier to say than do.

This leader and team represented a significant challenge, so we took small steps. It also helped that, at the time on the same island, I was coaching the other team who had a much lower performance history.

Throughout the coaching sessions, this second team showed great openness to improving their way of working. The team listened well and started to action learnings from their coaching.

One of the things the second team did was start to capture their actions and results visually. They used a simple system of index cards that the team leader converted into an Excel spread sheet and corresponding line graph.

The organisation often published information on large, flat screens all over the complex. When the team's progress was published it inadvertently created a kind of competition between the two teams. The second team was not known for this kind of progress. And their results prompted other areas of the business to ask the first team to publish theirs.

The power of their peers putting pressure on them motivated the first team to act, and slowly their toxicity towards adaption declined. However, it was difficult for them to completely lose the belief that their team was fine and that it was the other teams who needed to improve their performance; and I've found the tendency by one team to create this kind of myth about themselves a growing concern amongst business owners.

So, how does this myth present itself in an organisation? Let's find out.

I'm Okay—Everyone Else Needs To Change

Not recognising that a team needs to change its behaviour is a belief that any leader can develop at any level of performance.

This mindset typically appears because the leader and their team are good at what they do—they've been in their role for a long time and have mastered their role, knowing it inside out and back to front. Plus, they've used their skills and performed highly for a long time, and those results keep rolling in.

Then, slowly over time, their performance dwindles, so they point the finger of blame at other people—other teams. After all, they've performed well for years, so it couldn't possibly be them that's causing the problem. Could it?

With them stuck in this old way of thinking, it's very hard for them to realise that they need to change and adapt to an ever-changing world. Often brilliant executives and teams are not willing to change the way that they work because it's worked well for years.

When I worked in the banking sector years ago, we encountered a problem; it was profound, so it needed to be addressed quickly. Noting that this issue would be difficult to resolve, and at the same time could become too big to contain, I called a meeting with the heads of all the areas related to the incident.

Most heads accepted the meeting quickly, not questioning the need—except for one leader, that is, who said, "I don't know why you've included me in this; it's nothing to do with me or my team."

At the time I didn't care who was responsible; all I knew was that collectively we had to put out this fire before it became a raging inferno. My response to this leader was, "It's a real mystery how this problem occurred, but our priority is to get it sorted before it blows out of scale."

It was a hard road to travel. But collectively all teams worked together to resolve the issue. It turns out the problem existed between two teams, so no single group was to blame. However, without everyone's input, the problem would have escalated.

Resolving this issue and others like it is not about finding someone to blame. It is about understanding that, in this complex world, collectively using our wisdom to resolve problems is far more effective than operating in siloes, however 'high-performing.' Although, it is often easier said than done, with this myth often preventing problem resolution.

'Hand-Off' Culture

A 'hand-off' culture in an organisation is another way that this issue presents. Let's look at this in greater detail to gain a better understanding of this phenomenon.

You and your team are at the top of your game, and you have been for some time. You work in a large organisation, so you and your team are just one group amongst many. Therefore, when work is in progress, your team can quickly and efficiently do your part before handing off the work to another team.

Your priority is getting your part done, rather than the work as a whole. This approach has limited success and is magnified when a problem presents itself. As the high-performing, efficient team who has done their part, it is easier for you to assign failure to another team, rather than examine your own processes and admit that you and your team could make improvements.

This 'hand-off' culture leaves many teams high and dry and struggling to solve what is really a problem of the whole, rather than the parts. Meanwhile, the 'high- performing' team moves on to another project, never feeling the impact of the problem they have inadvertently contributed to.

This 'hand-off' culture exists in many workplaces, as many organisations have specific departments that carry out designated duties within confined role descriptions. If a problem occurs that falls outside of this role description, the standard approach is to pass it to the team with the appropriate roles. To make matters worse, this process is often automated, bypassing any opportunity for collaboration.

In many cases, the team handing off the work genuinely believes they are doing the right thing. In other cases, the problem is treated like the proverbial 'hot potato' and handed off swiftly. This approach (regardless of the intent) can result in a problem becoming difficult to resolve.

Team Bonus Structure

The way that organisations reward performance also encourages an 'us' and 'them' philosophy.

How?

Often in larger organisations, teams receive bonuses (at the completion of a project or a time period such as a financial year) when they perform well in their designated roles. Consequently, the way these bonuses are structured creates organisational silos where one team is so focused on their own results, they do not collaborate with another as the other team is perceived to be outside of their group[2] and may adversely affect the first team's bonus.

This is further magnified within teams where individuals may choose not to collaborate to protect their own bonus. The truth is we behave like we are rewarded, so if this myth is playing out for your organisation, take a good look at how individuals and teams are rewarded.

Avoiding Risks

Often, working collectively to achieve a common goal in an organisation can be very rewarding both personally and professionally. But sometimes the risks associated with collaboration also need to be weighed up.

I can recall working on a large project, years ago, in an international organisation. My team needed to purchase some very expensive infrastructure, and we had the choice of doing this as an individual team, which was the simplest approach with the result reflecting positively on the team, or we could collaborate with other teams within the organisation and jointly purchase a far more substantial piece of infrastructure that would be more of a lasting asset for the organisation.

However, the cost between the two pieces of infrastructure was significant—millions of dollars. So, my team weighed up the risks—we could buy a lesser piece of infrastructure and reap the rewards as a team, or we could rely on another team and buy a bigger, more powerful piece of infrastructure. But if the other teams failed to reach their goals and funding targets, then my team would overspend by millions.

Deciding that the risk was too great, my team opted to go it alone and buy our infrastructure independently.

Days later, we discovered that our decision paid off. The other teams had their projects cancelled. This meant that, if we had gone ahead with the joint purchase, my team would have been left footing the entire bill for the larger, more expensive infrastructure, which would have affected the business substantially. So, while my team wanted to take the enterprise approach on this occasion, it was best that we didn't.

Our act of self-protection was the best approach. And this happens a lot, resulting in many singular successes and denials of responsibility in organisations.

So, why does this happen so much? Let's look at four of the most profound reasons now.

It's Instinctive

It's a natural reaction for people to behave defensively when there's a problem because instinctively we see this as a threat.

Our instincts hail from our caveman days, where a threat can potentially remove us from our clan, and this, in turn, could represent a lack of food, water and shelter, which could result in death. So, if we put this instinctive nature into perspective in today's world, we see that admitting that you're at fault could jeopardise your job, which would see you removed from your position or clan—thus, in turn, affecting your ability to pay your mortgage, so you may lose the roof over your head (shelter), and you could have difficulties feeding yourself and finding water, which would affect your survival.

Subsequently, it's this fear of being ousted that sees you deny any responsibility for failure. If you think back to caveman days, being in a group equated to safety. Without that group, a sabre-toothed tiger could stalk and eat you because your defence is limited.

So, instead, we keep our heads down and deny all involvement—it's safer that way.

Safer Assigning Blame

Knowing that success comes from a team focus, many leaders will concentrate their efforts on their team and helping them to achieve results. This strategy not only reflects on the leader, who drives the team to perform, but also enables the team to remain focused and work towards a common purpose.

But, when a team can't maintain their high level of performance, and they start to slip, then it's difficult for a leader to admit that their team may need help. After all, their team has been at the top of their game for a long time, and they feel safe making risky decisions. If a leader then admits that their team is a part of a problem, then they may erode their team's confidence.

In a study on team performance conducted by Google, the quality that stood out in the highest-performing teams was psychological safety. If team members feel safe, then they take risks, speak their mind and unleash their creativity, which leads to great results and market breakthroughs.[3]

As a result, if a leader assigns blame to another team or doesn't admit to their team having a problem, then this enables the leader to maintain his team's focus. Plus, the leader avoids igniting the fight or flight response in their team, which can reduce analytical thinking capabilities and erode perspective.

Individual Achievement

Individual monetary targets such as remuneration and bonuses may drive individualistic behaviour instead of encouraging teams to work together and be enterprise driven. Of course, this depends on the company, but most companies offer their employees a yearly bonus after posting results.

For example, if you work in sales, then typically you'll receive a percentage bonus based on the amount of product that you've sold throughout the year. If your sales are high, then so will be your bonus.

Unfortunately, many companies don't offer team bonuses as frequently, which would promote a unified, enterprise-orientated culture. Many progressive organisations are starting to move over to this approach, so they encourage a cooperative culture rather than an individualistic one.

What's the cost of these behaviours?

Lost Market Share

Working with a particular client opened my eyes to how failing to recognise problems with a team can have a profound effect on a business. Let me explain.

This client went live with a brand-new system. The system itself was innovative, but the business hadn't thought about how each area of the system depended on each other. So, even though the system functioned, it wasn't to its fullest capacity as the business had focused on a small number of teams rather than all of them during the design, creation and launching stages.

While this approach works for developing a prototype, the system went live across the whole organisation and their customer base with many flaws.

These flaws resulted in disgruntled customers who felt that they were not being taken care of or looked after. Instead, they felt like they were being treated as a second thought, and this resulted in lost market share with these disgruntled customers going elsewhere.

System Failure

The client also called the entire a system a success, when in reality only sections of the system worked. By ignoring the other parts of the system—the ones that didn't operate effectively—this created more problems, as there were certain parts of the process that the customer couldn't carry out. Lacking the necessary connectors to make the system operate correctly resulted in system failure, and this in turn saw a high level of customer complaints made to the business.

Large organisations experience these types of difficulties frequently. When these companies experience system failure, a customer will go in search of resolution. But often what the customer experiences is far from a solution.

Recently, as a business and residential customer of one of these organisations, I experienced an issue with one of my services. Wanting to rectify the problem, I called customer service.

Even though I had called the number on my statement that related to this issue, I was transferred from department to department before finally finding someone who could help me. I explained and re-explained my problem to at least six people in between long periods of being on hold.

As someone with knowledge of and empathy for the complexity of large organisations, I worked to keep calm. I knew that, to each of the people I spoke to, this problem was brand new and they were just individual parts of a broken system, handing off that proverbial hot potato. However, inside I still felt frustrated, and found myself multi-tasking with an internet search for an alternative provider.

Everyone can relate to an experience like this, where even though we understand the complexities of multiple teams with different roles, we are still left feeling like we are being treated as a number, not a person.

So, how can teams effectively work together to achieve results?

> Imagine two fishermen in a boat fishing in a lake. The water is calm and smooth. Suddenly one end of the boat gets a hole in it. The fisherman at that end cries out in alarm and starts bailing. The fisherman at the other end breathes a sigh of relief: "Thank goodness that hole is not at MY end of the boat!"

Putting Out The Fire

The fire team in the Navy is an excellent example of how a team works together cohesively.

In a fire team, there is no individual person with the responsibility of putting out the fire. The fire team consists of five people—a leader to guide the team, an attack hose, a 'water-wall' hose and two hoses on the boundary cooling the compartment. Together, they ensure the fire is extinguished.

There are no individual performance indicators or goals, just the shared goals of putting out the fire. This philosophy flows throughout the navy.

Whenever there is an emergency on a ship, all teams work collectively towards the common goal of dealing with the emergency. If an individual or team can't perform their role, there is no finger of blame. Instead, all teams pull together to sort it out. In fact, taking a person or team out is a practice that is drilled regularly, as this is a likely scenario in a real-life situation.

So, a ship is essentially a system where everyone interdependently interacts and adapts to make the system work well. There's no use having one high-performing team in this system—all teams must perform well, and they must pull together. Otherwise, the ship won't function, and this can mean sinking, running aground or losing a battle.

Leadership on a warship is comparable to leadership of a business. Both leaders need to have certain skills—strong influence, quick thinking and a willingness to take measured risks. These leaders also need to view their people and teams as a part of a system.

Most importantly, it is the leader who is willing to be vulnerable, who possesses a willingness to learn, who also takes constructive criticism onboard and uses it to improve in an ever-changing world who will be highly effective.

By seeking guidance, this leader will continually grow, and they will develop a mindset that sees their team reach new heights of success. These teams will develop tactics, directions and bold plans that will enable them to find a way to win, regardless of the situation or the project.[4]

Key Takeaway

- Your organisation is a system that needs to be considered holistically, not as individual parts. Therefore, if you can see problems arise with other teams, then it's highly likely that you are contributing to those problems.

  "If you want to go fast, go alone. If you want to go far, go together."

  -- African Proverb

CHAPTER 10

"We Have All The Resources We Need Internally To Address Our Performance Issues; We Don't Need Any Outside Perspective"

The wake-up call sounded loud and clear with the 1940s bugle playing the familiar 'da da da dah' of the reveille at 5.45 am, and one by one the sailors climbed from their bunks, bleary-eyed and ready for action. Sharing their quarters with as many as 100 other men, each flattened their blankets and folded their bed into its designated niche, before they prepared for the day ahead.[1]

Meeting in the mess hall for breakfast at 8 am, the crew hurriedly ate, before heading off to meet their division leader to carry out their duties for the day. Responsibilities for the crew changed depending on the roles of the division and on the day; one day the crew may clean the deck, another they may check and clean artillery.

All crew relied on each other to carry out their responsibilities, and they used the resources on board the ship. Rarely did they need any outside help, except when working in a task group on an exercise or combat operation.

Navy life from the 1940s is very different to 2018. Today's modern warships rely on advanced technology.

Take for instance the USS Zumwalt, rolled out in 2013. This $3.5 billion ship's main objective is survival. It's fast, carries heavy firepower and relies on Linux. In fact, this ship's virtual data centre carries over 6 million lines of code.[2]

And yet, while the navy of today still rely on their own internal resources to address their performance, they also need an outside perspective to make them competitive in battle, much like an organisation.

Sometimes an outside perspective enables both the navy and an organisation to use their resources to their fullest capabilities. Without this help, these warships and businesses wouldn't achieve their goals.

Reflecting on these incidents, it can therefore be said that a leader who states they have all the resources they need and they don't need any outside help is technically sabotaging their own operation. In fact, it's a little like trying to sail a ship without a compass to guide you through the water. You can have a map and all the other tools needed to navigate, but if you don't have a compass that's working efficiently, then you won't complete your mission.

Automatically Following Orders

When you carry out the same job day in and day out for years, you start to carry out tasks automatically. It's a little like living through the 1990s movie *Groundhog Day* where you repeat the day over continuously as you're stuck in a time loop.

When you relive the same experiences, you don't realise when an issue presents itself. You've become complacent and switched off from the tasks at hand—you're simply working on autopilot.

For example, I can recall a time when I was aboard a naval ship years ago. We were on the bridge, and every now and then this random beeping noise would occur. When we first heard it, we investigated. But we didn't find any problem; there was no fire or any other sign of immediate danger that appeared obvious.

Eventually we discovered that by pushing this random grey button nearby when we heard the noise, the noise would stop. Then we wouldn't think anything more about the noise until it happened again.

Over time, we'd heard the noise so many times that we became complacent about it. In fact, it became a bit of a joke when someone new started in the bridge crew. The beeping noise would start, and the new person would ask, "What's that noise?"

We'd all respond, "What noise?"

The new person would repeat themselves, "That noise? Can't you hear it? It's driving me crazy."

Of course, we'd all say, "Nope, we cannot hear a thing." And, one of us would push the grey button.

Then one day someone from engineering was on the bridge when the noise went off. They suggested we investigate. We proceeded to test a bunch of theories and discovered that a series of events set off the beeping sound.

Interestingly, we also discovered that when we lifted the receiver—a form of communication on the bridge—this also set off an alarm in the engine room. Consequently, it was the engineer's outside perspective that solved our beeping problem on the bridge, and we solved the engine room's beeping sound issue also.

But without this outside perspective, it's doubtful that the bridge or engine room would have solved their beeping dilemma.

Having Needed Knowledge

In the past, the only reason you sought outside help was because you lacked the needed knowledge to complete tasks or finish a project. But you've grown and developed, expanding your knowledge and learning new skills continually. So, you now have all the knowledge you need, therefore you only need external bridge a knowledge gap if it occurs.

So you engage external help from people just like you that know a bit more. And while this is effective, it may not be giving you the perspective that you need to see the picture accurately. Let me explain.

It's a little like watching a magician performs a trick on television. You watch the magician perform the trick over and over, and every time you marvel at the magician's expertise.

But then you're shown the trick from a different camera angle, a different perspective, and as you watch the trick you realise that you can see how the trick is done. However, if you hadn't seen the trick from a different angle, then you would have never realised how the trick was performed.

Believing that anything is possible, Adelaide magician Vinh Giang is known for exposing how magic tricks are performed. Not so he could destroy the illusion, but so he could prove a very important point about perspective.

Vinh Giang believes that collaboration is the key to success in business. As such, he performs magic shows and then invites his audience to tell him how each of his tricks are done. By going through this process with his audience, Vinh Giang quickly teaches his onlookers the value of understanding perspective, and how this view solves problems.

While magic tricks appear extremely intricate and difficult to solve, once you understand how they are done you understand that the methods are quite simple. This same understanding of perspective can be applied to business, giving leaders exceptional clarity and insight.[3]

Devil's Advocate

Rather than embracing a range of perspectives from external sources outside of the business, a leader may believe that the only value external help can bring is the role of devil's advocate. The leader chooses to play this role instead, and takes the pessimistic approach, highlighting the faults and opposing new ideas. Playing devil's advocate for a leader is a far easier option than looking into possibilities.

By shutting down any new ideas, leaders reduce their level of risk and reduce the unknowns in a situation, thereby reducing the need to trust people. Often, the 'once bitten, twice shy approach' rears its head as well—where a leader may have trusted someone in the past, even years earlier, and this has back-fired with them still feeling the pain from that incident.

Leaders that play the devil's advocate typically prepare for the worst before it's even happened. They'll look for problems, such as suggesting that the cost will far outweigh the benefits, and this will demotivate others to try new ideas or to embrace innovation. They think they are saving the day with their perspective, when in fact they are encouraging a biased view.

So, why do leaders have this restricted view of bringing in an outside perspective?

Bad Consultation Experiences

Having dealt with consulting firms in the past, leaders feel they have not received value for their time or money. Prior experiences have left a bad taste in the leader's mouth. Consulting firms have come in and identified problems, but they have not shown leaders how they can resolve them.

So, leaders feel that these consulting firms have only carried out half of their job. And in some cases, have made the problem worse.

Having a high level of distrust means that many leaders fail to see the value of outside help. Thus, when leaders engage outside help, they cannot learn effectively, action the advice or connect the dots between the root cause and possible solutions. This high level of distrust prevents a leader from taking constructive feedback on board and being open to recognise something about themselves that was until this point unknown to them—this is a feature in the Johari Window, a business model that is used to enhance an individual's perception.[4]

GFC Panic

The Global Financial Crisis (GFC) increased the focus on risk, with many people within organisations facing the very real threat of losing their jobs, and organisations having to scale down their operations to survive. This financial crisis also made leaders and organisations more resistant to change as they used the GFC to compound their negative views when playing devil's advocate.[5]

Also, the outcomes from the GFC were systematic, which resulted in the need for the regulatory systems to change. This approach saw organisations having to review their practices and introduce tighter criteria. Consequently, reducing the level of risk, and raising greater awareness of the risk that was present, attracted a lot of focus, often preventing conversations about possibilities and the wider perspective so critical for business success.

Limited Perspective

As a leader, when you have a limited perspective, you only see what's in front of you. Therefore, it's difficult for you to understand new ways to solve a problem because you have a one-dimensional view—a solo perspective, your perspective.

But, if you had another point of view, another perspective because you asked someone else, then you would get a fresh interpretation of the problem.

Magician Vinh Giang proves this point by recording a magic trick that gives his viewers a limited or solo perspective. He then replays the recording of this trick to the live audience as he explains that, if he had done this trick 'live' on stage, then the audience would have had more than

2000 different perspectives from around the room. These perspectives would have enabled the audience to solve the trick, or as Vinh Giang calls it, the problem.[6]

Showing another recording of the same trick, from a different camera angle or perspective, Vinh Giang allows the audience to see that there are many more people in the room than first thought. The audience can also see other changes that they didn't notice in the first video because their attention focused solely on the trick, rather than what was happening in the background.

By exposing limited perspective for what it really is, Vinh Giang opens the audience's eyes to possibilities and shows them that problems which appear large often are very simple. This philosophy brings about an open-minded approach to problem solving and highlights that perspectives can change the way we solve problems.

So, what does having a limited perspective cost business?

Stagnation

When a business fails to push themselves out of their comfort zone and look at other possibilities, they stagnate. When a business stagnates, they are not only resisting change but also becoming content and focusing more on survival rather than on growth.[7]

When this scenario occurs, then the organisation forgets about their customer, they fail to engage their employees, and leaders cannot effectively lead their teams. The organisation struggles to attract and retain new talent. Instead, they simply exist and hope that any small adjustments they make will keep them ahead of their competition in a fast-changing world.

Lack Of Innovation

As a leader, you need to have a positive attitude. In fact, Intel co-founder Robert Noyce is known for referring to optimism as "an essential ingredient of innovation." If you have a negative view and play devil's advocate, then typically this belief will pass down to your team members.

Having a negative view in a workplace tends to demotivate team members, and this can cause them to focus more on security and stability and lack the willingness or ability to change and innovate.

This situation sees problems escalate, with the team and leader having no interest in resolving issues. Over time the department and organisation lose momentum, which can reduce customer numbers and eventually business turnover.

Lost Revenue

Businesses that don't keep up with change run the risk of missing opportunities as more nimble competitors move in. Plus, organisations can miss problems that can have a profound impact on the amount of revenue generated, which, in turn, can lead to insolvency.

As a coach, I see a lot of businesses finding it hard to keep up with change because they just can't move fast enough —these companies are large and cumbersome, and smaller, more nimble businesses are moving in and taking their market share.

I had a client a few years ago who had a very 'old-school' mindset, with out-dated processes and structures in place. So, when I was engaged to help this business improve its processes and way of working, they were not very accepting of my perspective. They saw my ideas as too 'out there.'

Sometime later, their customers started asking them for some of the ideas I had suggested. When this happened, then the business looked at what I had been suggesting months earlier with fresh eyes.

This situation then started to shift the beliefs of the business leader. However, the business had been too slow to respond, and it took time for them to then win back their customers who had since moved on.

You may remember a time when Apple dominated the smartphone market, and when it came to developing mobile applications, iOS development was always prioritised ahead of Android. Then Android numbers started to trend upwards, but most organisations still invested their development efforts in iOS.

The organisations which saw the change in consumer habits, however, paved the way for greater business growth by investing early in Android development capability. That meant they were not left behind when Android began to surpass Apple in the smartphone market.

This situation saw many companies fade into the background and eventually disappear, and all because they failed to look at a different perspective and embrace this change so that they could develop and grow.

My overall approach as a coach is to help businesses and organisations see their work from a different perspective. Often, these businesses have all the resources that they need, they just need to understand how to use these resources better and consider how different views can work for their company.

Bank Capability Study

I was asked to conduct an agile capability study for an Australian bank several years ago, which focused on the organisation's skills in this area and where they needed to improve. While the bank had the capabilities to carry out the study themselves, they just didn't have the time to focus on it. As it turned out, I gave them a fresh perspective and a different view of their capability and business operations.

After carrying out a lot of interviews and observing practices, I identified some key gaps in the system. This study led to the bank taking a new approach in upskilling their teams in agile practices.

So while a framework existed—one of the team members had already come up with the initial idea—she also admitted that she had no idea how to implement the concept. It took my unique perspective to put this framework into action.

Disney's Creativity Strategy

Years ago, Disney took what everyone called a leap of faith—CEO Robert Igar purchased Pixar for a colossal $7.4 billion.

Everyone thought he was crazy. After all, Disney was animation-focused with their classic characters such as Mickey and Minnie Mouse being some of the best known in the industry.

But Disney knew that every industry changes, and, to keep at the top of the performance ladder, the company had to adapt to this change and adopt an innovative strategy.[8]

The risk paid off for the Disney CEO, and a few years later he bought Marvel Entertainment for $4 billion. Then the company purchased Lucasfilm for a similar figure a few years later. These moves not only saw Disney diversify their market share but also kept the business venture alive and active in an ever-changing world.

Disney's creativity strategy is entirely dependent on alternate perspectives. When a new idea is floated, the first thing they do is think about everything good about the idea and build on it.

They call this the 'dream room.' Only after this, do they focus on the potential risks, which then leads to a realistic discussion. Disney learned a long time ago that if you criticise any idea early enough in the process it has no chance to grow at all.

Let The Compass Guide You

Learning is continual, it never stops. As a leader, you need to be willing to learn and listen all the time. You also need to be willing to accept guidance and embrace the perspectives of others.

You may not always agree with these perspectives but keeping your mind open to possibilities enables you to gain greater insight. You may even see opportunities that take your organisation and team to higher levels of performance than you ever thought possible.

As a leader, keep your compass—your business navigation tools—up-to-date and in good working order.

You never know when you will need these to guide you through turbulent waters.

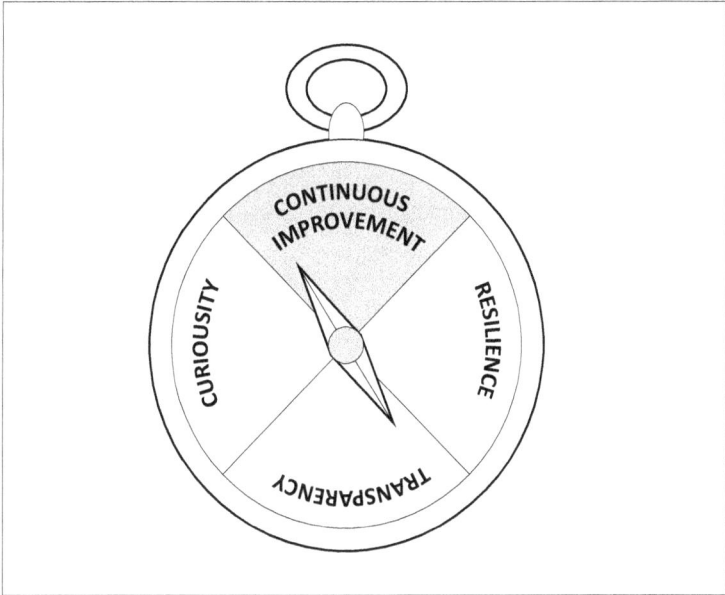

By embracing opportunities when they present themselves, your team and organisation will keep on top of their game. You will notice changes in the market and come up with ways to expand your perspective so that you resolve problems and embrace changes to maximise business opportunities and profits.

Key Takeaways

- In the new and emerging world, it's vital that you know that you don't have to do it all on your own.

While this strategy may have worked in the past, it won't work now. The pace of change is way too fast.

- The leader of the future is the person who integrates internal resources with external skills and knowledge to take meaningful action. This balanced view will lead to world-class results.

"There's no earthly way of knowing which direction we are going. There's no way of knowing where we're rowing or which way the river's flowing."

-- Willy Wonka and the Chocolate Factory

If this book has resonated with you, and you seek the definitive 'compass' that will take your performance culture to a world-class level, then visit www.HighPerformanceCulturePartners.com.au/Consult to book a Complimentary Performance Strategy Session (value $795.00).

REFERENCES

Chapter 1

[1] Daffern, Josh. *How Do You Catch a Monkey? (The Trap We Humans Fall For).* Patheos.com 2015.

[2] *Web Finance Inc. Taylorism. Business Dictionary.com 2018.*

[3] McLachlan, Andrew. *Notes and Queries: Who Invented Traffic Lights and Where Were the First Ones Situated?* Guardian.co.uk 2011.

[4] Wikipedia. Website. https://en.wikipedia.org/wiki/Roundabout.

Chapter 2

[1] Lyons, Suzannah. *Tropical Cyclone Tracey: December 25, 1974.* ABC.net.au 2014.

[2] Royal Australian Navy News. *Darwin Edition. Vol 18. No.1.* Navy.gov.au 1974.

[3] McRaney, David. *The Sunken Cost Fallacy.* YouAreNotSoSmart.com 2011.

[4] Facebook Apps. *Farmville2. Facebook.com 2018.*

[5] Graft, Kris. *500 Games Launched Per Day.* Gameasutra.com 2015.

[6] Kahneman, Daniel. *Thinking Fast and Slow.* Farrar, Straus & Giroux New York 2011.

[7] Zhang, Michael. *A Brief History of Kodak: The Rise and Fall of a Camera Giant.* PetaPixel.com 2018.

[8] Dan, Avi. *Kodak Failed By Asking The Wrong Market Question.* Golbal.Forbes.com 2012.

[9] Ludowig, Kirsten. *For CEOs, Uncertainty is the Only Certainty.* Golbal.handelsblatt.com 2017.

Chapter 3

[1] Morris, Jane. *The Guggenheim Bilbao 20 Years Later: How a Museum Transformed a City.* News.artnet.com 2017.

[2] Phaidon. *Buildings That Changed the World – The Guggenheim Museum Bilbao. Au.phaidon.com 2012.*

[3] Mendelsohn, Ashley. *How Analog and Digital Came Together in the 1990s Creation of the Guggenheim Museum Bilbao.* Guggenheim.org 2017.

[4] Mercandetti, Michael. *Wound Healing and Repair.* Emedicine. medscape.com 2017.

[5] Project Smart. *The Standish Group Chaos Report.* Projectsmart. co.uk 2014.

[6] Covey, Stephen. *The Speed of Trust.* Play.Google.com 2018.

[7] Hardy-Vallee Benoit. *The Cost of Bad Project Management.* News.gallup.com 2012.

Chapter 4

[1] Willink, Joko and Babin, Leif. *Extreme Ownership.* MacMillian Publishers Australia 2018.

[2] Hodgson, Matthew. *Why Spotify's Agile Patterns Work and Why You Shouldn't Copy and Paste Them.* Zenexmachina.wordpress. com 2017.

[3] Jager, Chris. *Why Starbucks Failed in Australia.* Lifehacker.com 2018.

[4] Cain, Aine. *A Day In The Life Of Billionaire Richard Branson. BusinessInsider.com.au 2018.*

[5] Branson, Richard. *My (Usual) Daily Routine.* Virgin.com 2017.

[6] PCMA Convening Leaders 2019. *Mastery Is Magic: Vinh Giang.* Conveningleaders.org 2018.

Chapter 5

[1] BBC Scotland. *The Arnish Lighthouse.* BBC.co.uk 2006.

[2] Caldwell, Felicity. *Delayed Queensland Government Project More Than Doubles in Cost. BrisbaneTimes.com.au 2018.*

[3] Welch, Dylan. *$171m Budget Blow-Out Takes the Shine Off ASIO's New HQ.* SMH.com.au 2012.

[4] Kaye, Sharon. *William Of Ockham.* IEP.utm.edu 2018.

[5] WDD Staff. *Occam's Razor: A Great Principle for Designers.* Webdesignerdepot.com 2018.

[6] Lencioni, Patrick M. *The Advantage: Why Organizational Health Trumps Everything Else In Business.* John Wiley & Sons 2012.

Chapter 6

[1] Wilkins, Muriel Maignan. *Signs That You're a Micromanager.* HBR.org 2014.

[2] Henshall, Adam. *Taylorism and the History of Process: 6 Key Thinkers You Should Know. Process.st 2018.*

[3] Pink, Daniel. *Drive: The Surprising Truth About What Motivates Us.* New York: Riverhead Books. 2009.

[4] Huichun, Yu and Miller, Peter. *Leadership Style: The X Generation & Baby Boomer Compared to Different Cultural Context.* epubs. scu.edu.au 2005.

[5] Martin, Gary. *How Is Presenteeism Affecting Your Workplace?* Hrmonline.com.au 2018.

[6] Atlassian. *You Waste A Lot Of Time At Work.* Atlassian.com 2018.

[7] D'Onfro, Jillian. *The Truth About Google's Famous '20% Time' Policy.* Businessinsdier.com.au 2015.

[8] Lindsay, Greg. *Yahoo Says That Killing Working From Home Is Turning Out Perfectly.* Fastcompany.com 2013.

[9] Peck, Emily. *Proof That Working From Home Is Here To Stay: Even Yahoo Does It.* Huffingtonpost.com.au 2017.

Chapter 7

[1] NASA History. *The First Flight of Space Shuttle Challenger.* Nasa.gov 2018.

[2] A&E Television Networks. *Challenger. History.com 2018.*

[3] Wall, Mike. *Challenger Disaster 30 Years Ago Shocked the World, Changed NASA.* Space.com 2018.

[4] Harris, Robin. *Death by PowerPoint.* Zdnet.com 2010.

[5] Timmons, Milt. *The Anatomy of Power.* Miltontimmons.com 2018.

[6] Spradlin, Dwayne. *Are You Solving the Right Problem?* HBR.org 2012.

[7] Gleeson, Brent. *The Silo Mentality: How To Break Down The Barriers.* Forbes.com 2013.

[8] Titanic Universe. *Titanic History.* TitanicUniverse.com 2013.

Chapter 8

[1] Gupta, Gaurav. *Percentage Alignment Amongst Management Teams.* Industyweek.com 2009.

[2] Pilcher, Jeffry. *Say It Again: Messages Are More Effective When Repeated.* TheFinancialBrand.com 2018.

Chapter 9

[1] Murphy, Mark. *The Dunning-Kruger Effect Shows Why Some People Think They're Great Even When Their Work Is Terrible.* Forbes.com 2017.

[2] Sessoms, Gail. *What are Organizational Silos? Yourbusiness. azcentral.com 2018.*

[3] Delizonna, Laura. *High-Performing Teams Need Psychological Safety.* Hbr.org 2017.

[4] Willink, Jocko and Babin, Leif. *Extreme Ownership: How U.S Navy Seals Lead and Win.* St Martin's Press. New York 2015.

Chapter 10

[1] Alison. *Life On A World War II Battleship.* Vistitpearlharbor.org 2016.

[2] *Gallagher, Sean. The Navy's Newest Warship Is Powered By Linux. Arstechnica.com 2013.*

[3] Giang, Vinh. *Keynote Speaker.* Vinhgiang.com 2018.

[4] Communication Theory. *The Johari Window Model.* Coomunicationtheory.org 2018.

[5] Juneja, Prachi. *Global Financial Crisis and Organizational Change.* Managementstudyguide.com 2015.

[6] Giang, Vinh. *Perspective.* Youtube.com 2015.

[7] Garner, Janine. *The Business of Stagnation: Status Quo and Change Resistance.* TheCEOmagazine.com 2016.

[8] Govindarajan, Vijay. *How Disney found Its Way Back To Creative Success.* Hbr.org 2016.

NOTES

NOTES

www.ingramcontent.com/pod-product-compliance
Lightning Source LLC
Chambersburg PA
CBHW060556200326
41521CB00007B/586